© 2015 William H. Stone

All rights reserved. No portion of this book may be reproduced, stored in a retrieval system, or transmitted in any form or in any means-electronic, mechanical, photocopy, recording, scanning, or other-except for brief quotations in critical reviews or articles, without the prior written permission of the publisher.

Cover: the Lorenz attractor, with its distinctive butterfly shape, is an icon of chaos theory. The teaching of Chaos theory helped organize the ideas expressed in this book.

Cover design by Craig Casey, President and Creative Director, workshop-marketing.com

ISBN 100692614966
ISBN 13 9780692614969

Dedication and Expression of Appreciation

This book grew from my involvement with my work at the MES Foundation under the direction of Richard Pierce and Scottie Higgins, the development of Promising Futures, and through countless workshops for people who had lost their jobs. My first thanks goes to them. At the MES Foundation I worked with the most outstanding group of professionals I could ever hope to work with. They included Crisanne Blackie, Janet Etzel, Robin Murphy, Betty Ryder, and especially Bill Webb. Their influence is found throughout this book.

Over the course of my efforts to organize my ideas one source of support stands out: Thank you, Catherine.

Table of Contents

Foreword by Jim Peacock, CDF	*viii*
Introduction by Crisanne Kadamus Blackie, NCCC, Director, Career Center, University of Maine	*x*
Organizing Serendipity in a Turbulent Economy: Why Read This Book.	1
Floating on the Sea of Serendipity: Getting Ready to take Action	5
Careers in a Chaotic World: The Context for Using Your Scanner	12
The Four Scans	17
Order Out of Chaos	21
The First Scan: Building Momentum and Living Your Commitment to Your Future	22
The Second Scan: Knowing What Matters to You in the Work That You Do	28
The Third Scan: Intentional Learning and Synthesis	48
The Fourth Scan: Building Synergistic Relationships and Reaching Out to the World With All That You Have to Offer	56

The Plan: How to Use What You Have Learned About Chaos, Systems, and the Four Scans	65
Conclusion: The Seeds of Success Exist Within You	69
Activities Section	70
• Activity One: Reality Check	70
• Activity Two: Internal and External Scan	74
• Activity Three: Feelings Scale	87
• Activity Four: Your "Go-for-It Gauge"	91
• Activity Five: Tips for Momentum Building	95
• Activity Six: Tuning your Scanner with an Awareness of Your Temperament Preferences	104
• Activity Seven: Tuning Your Scanner with a Career Experience Timeline	108
• Activity Eight: Tuning Your Scanner with Your Ideal Job Description	112
• Activity Nine: Your 30-Second Commercial	114
• Activity Ten: How to Do Cold Calls	116

Worksheets and Ideas to Help Manage Your Career and Your Life	119
• *The Keys to Your Future*	119
• *Opportunities Are Everywhere*	122
• *How People Really Get Jobs*	126
• *Effective Networking Techniques*	128
• *Some Ideas for Creating Your Resume*	131
• *Accomplishment Statements for Effective Resumes*	133
• *Professional Summary for Effective Resumes*	135
• *Action Verbs for Resumes and Interviews*	138
• *Interviewing Skills*	144
• *What prospective Employers Want to Know about You*	145
• *The Promising Futures Axioms for Salary Negotiations*	148
• *Creating a Business Card*	151
• *Stages of Change Often Encountered by*	

Workers Making an Unplanned Career Change	155
• *After-the-Interview Thank You Note Examples*	156
• A Word about LinkedIn and Facebook	159
Appendices:	161
• Applying the Science of Chaos to Managing Your Career	161
• Re-Careering After 50: Organizing Serendipity for Those with Lots of Experience	173
About the Author	189

**Foreword by Jim Peacock, CDF
Past President, Maine Career Development Association, Career Development Facilitator Instructor www.Peak-Careers.com**

Chaos. Serendipity. Happenstance. Luck. This IS how people find work throughout their career development. I am a huge fan of the Happenstance Learning Theory and my personal philosophy is what I call "Intentional serendipity." You need to be "intentional" and take action and then be open to opportunities that you create. Chaos theory has many crossovers.

I love that this book not only explains how chaos is normal in our lives and how you can use it to create your opportunities, but also weaves specific activities throughout to help formulate your thinking and take action in your career development.

Bill Stone has a great sense of humor that trickles out when you least expect it, and he has a deep respect for all people and all jobs that is too often missing in other books I read. His practical advice on how to "scan" for information on yourself, businesses, opportunities, and people in your network gives you a comprehensive format to accelerate your career development.

If you have been wondering why you have not been able to find a new job, or feel that your life is out of control and you can't figure out how to rein it in, or you would just like a practical, up-to-date overview of how to find work that fits you, start reading this book.

Introduction
Crisanne Kadamus Blackie, NCCC
Director, Career Center, University of Maine

The concept of the relationship between chaos theory and careers has been an evolving conversation between Bill and I for the past 20 years. His thoroughness of thought has brought him to the point of publishing "Chaos, Creativity and Careers". These ideas and exercise have been a great influence as to the way I view career counseling. To help a client experience the "ah ha" moment when (s)he really believes that (s)he can do this, can move forward and can make a plan with intentionality is extremely rewarding. Understanding how systems form and evolve helps to explain how one can make a change, recognize opportunities and create synergistic relationships.

These concepts will help career practitioners and career decision makers move forward with agility and resilience. Learning the process and repeating it over and over teaches adaptability. As careers evolve and change, one needs the ability to be nimble and continually reinvent. Learning these skills is the key to taking the uncertainty out of your future. I encourage you to embrace this book and begin to scan. Once you try this, it will change the way you view the world.

Organizing Serendipity in a Turbulent Economy: Why Read this Book

Early in my career of helping others I interviewed a young man in my guidance office. He was not certain why he was there, why he received a pass to speak to a guidance counselor, and whether he was in trouble. I simply wanted to know about his plans for the future so I came right to the point. I asked him what he planned to do after school. He thought for a minute and responded, "I guess I'll go home and eat supper." Years later I was conducting a workshop for administrative staff members who had just been laid off from their jobs at a hospital. One woman arrived late and sat with the group. As I welcomed her the tears welled up in her eyes and she said, "I am 43 years old. What am I going to do?" I write this book for all of those folks who are at some sort of crossroads, self-imposed or otherwise.

This book will help you organize your luck. Using the principles I outline here will help you organize your thoughts and focus on the tasks you need to complete in order to manage your career growth. Career growth does not happen by chance, but rather by the relentless drive of your career self-concept to self-organize. I call it "organizing serendipity." Serendipity refers to the discovery of good things—seemingly by accident. In reality, there is no serendipity. There is only the force of self-organization. Self-organization is the naturally occurring process of self-assembly that occurs within any open system. Weather systems, for example, swirl about in a seeming random fashion until they gather enough heat, moisture, and direction to begin to form the classic comma-shaped cloud patterns we see on the nightly weather report. All weather systems want to be hurricanes when they grow up, but there is so much conflicting "data," hurricanes are hard to form. Self-organization is found in areas such as economics, sociology, chemistry, etc. Whenever elements began to interact they naturally self-organize.

Self-organization continues throughout your periods of career growth, stagnation, or prolonged unemployment. Learning to manage the self-organization process will lead to your serendipity. If you want to get lucky get busy!

Active self-awareness (our capacity for introspection) is the key to organizing serendipity. Awareness of:

- What you are willing to do to help yourself,
- What matters to you in the work that you do,
- How you will build the knowledge base that you need, and
- How you will meet the people you need to know.

Throughout this book I refer to refining and using your self-awareness as scanner tuning. Scanner tuning is the deliberate effort to know what you are looking for, the belief that you can find it if you try, the desire to learn all you can about your choices, and then to keep busy by looking. Through the following pages I also details four scans to help you organize the turbulence in your career and find the order hidden beneath the chaos: (1) Knowing what you're willing to do, (2) knowing what matters to you in the work that you do, (3) synthesizing new knowledge about yourself and your work, and (4) building synergistic relationships. I'll define these later.

In this book I offer material for a variety of audiences.

- If you're a **counselor**, understanding self-organizing systems helps you organize counseling interventions and discover exercises to use in your practice.

- If you're **employed** and looking for ways to enhance your career, this book keeps you focused on the best path. You can prepare to spot opportunities and avoid the wrong job.

- If you're **unemployed** and want to be re-employed, you can discover new opportunities right under your nose.

- If you're **re-careering** later in your working life, you can discover the skills that will keep you competitive.

- If you're a **student** building a portfolio, you can organize a rich profile for future employers or even build your own entrepreneurial enterprise.

- If you're **thinking about college** but not sure what to study, you can build sensitivity to the things that will be important to you in your future employment. That helps you discover majors that could lead to a dream job.

Regardless of your role building career opportunities for yourself or for others, career opportunities generally means working for one employer but it could include a project-based employment where you might tackle problems as an independent consultant, bringing some job insecurity, but also career mobility and higher salaries. Commanding the agility to move from among several employers and perhaps re-careering, will thus replace retention, and the higher salaries will compensate, in part, for the reduced benefits. If you are re-careering after 50, you face the threat of age discrimination, and in all likelihood you will work in a small business—probably one you start. To join the ranks of the newly independent worker, you need to develop increased skill agility and learn to serve as your own benefits manager and financial planner.

This book helps you take an *entrepreneurial* approach to managing your talents and organizing your potential for learning new skills as you prepare to work for companies that flourish by managing a "just-in-time" work force. As a *career entrepreneur*, you are in business for yourself and you take responsibility for selling your services. You may service one "customer" (if you plan to take a job with one organization) or you may plan to hang out your shingle and offer your services to multiple clients. Regardless of whether you are the butcher, baker, candlestick maker, taking responsibility for your career makes you a career entrepreneur.

Becoming such a *career entrepreneur* with the skills to *organize serendipity* requires mastery of new career models. These new models certainly make use of established career management practices, but your approach also requires systematic management of career turbulence. Develop a keen sense of self-awareness—building a vocabulary to describe what matters to you in the work that you do and your preferred personality style. Self-awareness enhances situational awareness.

This book explains the science that supports my approach, a narrative to help you focus on managing your career, and a set of exercises to help create self-awareness. The exercises and the narrative will help you gain confidence in my ideas. If you employ these principles and organize your serendipity, chaos theory tells us that you will succeed.

Floating on the Sea of Serendipity: Getting Ready to Take Action

Just when everything seems to be going pretty well, it all changes. Then again, when things aren't going so well, it also changes.

Life seems like we are sticks in a stream, floating one way, then another, sometimes drifting in a tranquil back eddy, other times crashing through the rocks with the current. The flow of circumstances that makes up our careers, like the stream, continues despite our efforts. Sometimes it's a dribble; sometimes it's a rampaging river. Good fortune in our careers often seems to be left to serendipity. We do not, however, need to be entirely adrift.

There are patterns within the turbulence of our careers, and we do affect the way those patterns unfold. While good fortune in our careers may seem to be left to serendipity, we can organize serendipity.

Look at the stream. You will notice we cannot always predict just where the stick will be at any time or necessarily when it will be swept into the current. If we look at the anatomy of the stream, however, we see that certain patterns in the stream bottom repeat themselves, and ripples look pretty much the same up and down our stream.

If you are a canoeist, you have learned how to "read" the water's surface. A "V" that points down the stream means safe passage. The water is passing between two rocks, and you might get through. A "V" that points up the stream means the water is going around a rock just below the surface. Avoid it!

The patterns in our careers tend to reoccur much like patterns in the stream. You may never know when any characteristic will appear, but you can learn to control those elements of your behavior that encourage the good patterns and avoid bad patterns. Much like the stream is organized around the force of the current and the structure of the stream bottom, so your career organizes itself around your attitude and the personal behaviors that you tend to repeat within the work environments you have chosen.

When we watch the stream, we cannot predict with certainty where any given molecule of water will be at any particular time in the future, but we can see where the molecules tend to go. Likewise, we cannot predict what may happen to us at any moment in our working lives, but we can learn to predict the tendencies for certain things to happen.

This book is about shaping the tendencies that lead to good fortune or serendipity in your career by managing your thoughts and behaviors. Through a process of self-examination, I believe you can learn to build a strong tendency to succeed. Just as you can learn to scan the water for certain features and guide your canoe accordingly, learning to scan your attitudes, work behaviors, and your environment, and to act accordingly, helps build career success.

The More You Know the More You See

Purposefully scanning our attitudes, work behaviors, and environment is the basic skill I teach you in this book. Learning to think about our thinking is called *metacognition*. I hope to teach you to think and observe your own thinking about your attitudes and work behaviors first, and then the environment and how you think about it. Understanding yourself precedes understanding your environment. It is a bit like observing yourself from outside your body and watching what you think, feel, and do. This *metacognitive* process, or self-observation, leads to four key benefits:

1) Understanding the behavior patterns that have brought you to where you are today.

2) Knowing one's self and the different types of tasks you prefer.

3) Shaping strategies for life patterns you want to build for yourself.

4) Understanding your relationship with the world around you.

In the simplest terms, **the better you understand what is important to you in the work you do, the more opportunities you will see.** Keep that in mind as you read this guide to shaping your thoughts about your career growth, and you will gain a good deal from the material I offer. The basic skill I teach you in this book is scanner tuning.

Scanner Tuning

If we scan the brook, we know the stream organizes itself around elements such as the strength of the current and the nature of the streambed. If we scan for those elements, we can understand how the patterns in the stream emerge and take shape.

Our career scanners are already tuned both by beliefs about ourselves and by how we believe we relate to the world. You must ask yourself, "Am I tuned to the success I want, or am I tuned to the life I have resigned myself to live?"

You will organize your life around how you think your life is supposed to be. Want a different life? Tune your scanner to the way you want your life to be and you will organize your life accordingly. The self-organizing drive of systems tells us that it has to happen. Success starts with knowing what you are looking for, or tuning your scanner to the success you want for yourself.

A popular optical illusion may help you understand scanner tuning. Please read the sentence in the triangle below.

Now count the number of times the word "the" appears. Most of us fill in the blank and ignore the second "the." Our scanner is tuned to complete the sentence. We tend not to examine each word. Now that you know the word "the" appears twice, your scanner is tuned to spot it.

We have all experienced scanner tuning. Perhaps you bought a new car with an exotic color only to realize cars like yours were everywhere. Maybe you learned about a new food only to find it had been around you all along. *YouTube* offers a particular compelling example with a puzzle involving a *Double-Dutch Brain Game* jump rope demonstration at https://www.youtube.com/watch?v=iiEzf3J4iFk.

Your career scanner works just like the two examples above. Scanner tuning means you intentionally scan yourself (*metacognition – think about your thinking!*) and your environment, and then intentionally filter the sort of information you look for to create new ideas. We have all learned to filter information according to our genetic make-up, the way we have been raised, and what we have learned as we matured. This scanner you have created is naturally tuned and in use, even as you read these paragraphs.

Since you have been busy tuning your own scanner, did you tune your scanner intentionally or did you let the world around you decide the sort of life you would live for yourself? Please know that you can take charge of your own scanner tuning. Taking charge will mean the difference between living your dream or resigning yourself to live some compromise you did not intend to make.

I must offer you one word of warning: Intentionally tuning your scanner is harder than letting others tune it for you. Living life intentionally brings greater rewards, but it also requires greater effort.

You are already intentionally tuning your scanner. You did, after all, pick up this book to learn something to help your career.

Congratulations. You have already taken responsibility for your own scanner tuning success.

Scanner tuning is about learning to be intuitive. Intuition essentially is pattern recognition. When we have a "hunch" about something, the "hunch" represents our efforts to organize little bits of information into some sort of useful pattern. When those bits of information "click" into place, we may have a déjà vu experience, or the "gut" instinct that we are making a good decision.

While intuition may seem like an inelegant way to make decisions, our intuition gains authority as we gather more and more data about our environment and ourselves. As we scan our environment and ourselves gathering this data, we create a vibrant repertoire of patterns to begin to intuitively understand the attitudes and behaviors that shape more satisfying careers.

Organizing serendipity thus means we pursue the hard work of self-understanding, remaining diligent as we scan our surroundings, and using our well-developed intuition to spot opportunities. It may seem ironic, but scientists who use logic to make great discoveries tend to stumble onto their revelations rather unexpectedly. In other words, they used their analytical skills to build the intuition they needed to realize the breakthroughs we all depend on.

Once you begin to employ our intuitively-based approach to career management, which I call scanner tuning, your dreams must come true.

The legendary golfer Gary Player is reputed to have said, "The more I practice, the luckier I get." If you keep practicing the scanning process, internally and externally, you will find that your "career luck" improves. This practicing process is what I call "organizing serendipity." You organize serendipity by performing these scans:

I   Internally
　　1) Accepting responsibility for your destiny and believing you can make a contribution to the world around you.
　　2) Learning about what matters to you in life and on the job.
II Externally
　　3) Becoming an intentional learner.
　　4) Building mutually beneficial relationships with those around you.

The more you practice using these scans, the more your outlook will expand and change, and the more those career-enhancing serendipitous opportunities will occur. You will make your own "luck" toward building the sort of career you want.

At this point, you may want to do Activity Two: Internal and External Scan

Careers in a Chaotic World: The Context for Using Your Scanner

Our working world is characterized by turbulence. All of us live in a river of rapidly flowing, tumultuous, and fluid information. When you are just familiarizing yourself with a task, you are flooded with new information and new expectations that cause you to reframe your working role—a result of exchanging information with the environment.

We live and work on the edge of chaos. The career systems we have experienced are short-lived, often disrupted, and then reformed in ways that are difficult to determine. In the most cynical terms, the job you now have will change significantly and then disappear. Perhaps you should view this chronic disappearing act as the emergence of new opportunities. If you maintain your career agility by keeping your scanner tuned, you can actually enjoy these new them.

With the rapid exchange of information and changes in technology, the fundamentals of career planning remain the same. You still need to believe in yourself, know what you do best, learn all you can, and network. As we examine the trends that we believe we see, we can learn to ask ourselves the appropriate growth questions that will help us tune our scanner.

What You Need to Know About Chaos Theory and Systems Thinking, and Why You Should Care to Know

> *"There are no coincidences." Joe Leaphorn, Tony Hillerman Character*

Earlier, I made the bold claim that once you begin to employ your intuitively based approach to career management—called scanner tuning—your dreams have to come true. It is inevitable. If you use the four scans you will succeed in your efforts to "organize serendipity."

Next comes the science of self-organizing systems and the science of chaos theory to explain your inevitable success. Systems, such as your career, consist of many little things that work together to make a big thing that has purpose. Your career consists of all your skills and values that combine to make up your unique work patterns.

As you grow and learn, your work patterns adapt to new information. Chaos theory explains what happens when something disrupts your work patterns, such as a lay-off or the realization that you need a career change.

The primary lesson of systems thinking and chaos theory is that if you intentionally use all of the ideas I present in this book, you have to achieve the type of career you want. If you follow what I outline here, things will change the way you make them change, for better or for worse, depending on what you really want to have happen. What I will tell you about these two very profound sets of ideas (systems thinking and chaos theory) will give you three key mindsets:

1. Confidence in your ability to master your own destiny—even to the point of creating your own good luck, or "organizing serendipity" as I like to say.
2. Assurance that what I tell you here will work.
3. Certainty that if you follow other good career development models, they will work as well.

It is all about discipline over impulse.

Use a reliable system like mine and then stick with it. It must work for you. Chaos theory and systems thinking show us that you cannot fail.

Reviewing what can we learn from systems thinking and chaos theory, and how they will help us build our careers

1. *Systems are self-organized. Every system organizes around a very few basic elements. Weather systems organize around heat and moisture. Your career organizes around what you believe about your career and the environment where you work.*
2. *You cannot predict the future with certainty because you don't know all the events that lead into the future—the same way you cannot predict the weather with absolute certainty. You can, however, draw from the trends you observe from your past successes in order to influence your future.*
3. *Little changes, conscientiously applied over time, bring profound impact to large systems. The flapping of a butterfly's wing in China can bring a tornado to Texas; likewise, consistent efforts to improve your performance can change the whole company. When, by chance, Fleming noticed his bacteria was dying it led to the discovery of penicillin and a seismic shift in the way we treat disease. You can change any company by changing your behavior.*
4. *You cannot predict when a system will accept any change. You can, however, prepare to capitalize on change.*
5. *When things do change, they tend to change in a hurry.*
6. *Systems cannot remain stable; certainty and security can be*

ominous harbingers of impending collapse.
7. *Everything is connected to everything else. Your attitude right now, your daily work, the people you immediately work with, your company, your industry, our national economy, and global trade are all connected; when you move, it all moves -- at least for you.*
8. *We need enough regularity in our lives to be systematic, but enough chaos in order to create and grow.*

Once more, with gusto: Systems are self-organized. Every system organizes around a very few basic elements. Weather systems organize around heat and moisture. Your career organizes around what you believe about your career.

What we believe about ourselves as workers is a career system. Systems are made up of elements that have something in common. Elements of our career systems include what we believe about our effectiveness as workers; our favorite skills; our career values; the way we like to learn and process information; and the way we build relationships with others.

Features of our career systems:

- We gather information about the world around us.
- We form opinions about what works and what does not work for us.
- We build models for our behavior that guide us in the future, and then we behave according to those models.
- As we gain experience, some of the models we build compete with each other.
- Some of our opinions about what works for us are correct and some are erroneous. Like superstitions, our opinions form because we connect results to some action we took. Sometimes the connection between the results and the action we took is there; sometimes it is not there.
- Changing superstitions is difficult.

How knowing all of this helps you plan your career according to what we have explored so far...

- Your career is a system made up of several beliefs that influence your career behaviors.
- You may not know the basic elements that are the foundation for those beliefs, but you can observe your previous patterns of success and begin to get a sense out of what elements drive your career.
- Your career is also subject to the whims of sudden change, but even within those seemingly chaotic patterns, there is order.
- While you may not be able to predict the changes in your career, you can develop four scans that will help you scan the environment and prepare yourself to navigate change.
- You will organize your career around what you believe about your ability to contribute, what you think matters to you, how you learn, and the relationships you form. Your values serve as a compass to guide you through change.
- By tending to your scans, you can even initiate change.

The Four Scans

I have organized the scanner tuning process around two major scans, and broken each of these into two more scans. First, you make two scans of yourself (internal) and then you make two scans of your environment (external) for a total of four scans. You have been using these scans to select the information that you see and the information that you let through to influence your decision-making process. I present the scans as a list but in reality they occur concurrently and impact each other.

Internal Scans

Scan One) Scan your willingness to take responsibility for your career: Are you building personal commitment momentum toward your success? Do you believe that you are responsible for your own career success?

Scan Two) Scan your values, skills, and interest so that you know what matters to you: Do you know what matters to you in the work that you do? Is the work that you do congruent with your values and the skills you prefer to use?

Environment Scans

Scan Three) Scan for information about your career and your willingness to seek out new learning experiences: Are you intentional about your learning and synthesis process? Do you take responsibility for your own learning?

Scan Four) Scan for opportunities to build mutually beneficial relationships: Are you building networks and synergy? Do you understand that the relationships you build will create opportunities for you and for those around you?

For the sake of brevity, let's call the four scans...

Scan One) Momentum Building
Scan Two) Knowing What Matters
Scan Three) Synthesizing Information
Scan Four) Building Synergistic Relationships

You might think of this scanning process as a funnel, with the four scans gathering and filtering information. The information that makes its way through the scans and down the funnel influences your beliefs about your future career success.

As you scan, you gather information about yourself and your environment. You gather the information and filter it according to what you believe about your level of confidence, what you believe matters to you in the work you do, your ability to learn, and the mutually beneficial relationships you have formed.

Some items you simply won't notice; some you will consider and discard. Other items of information will become part of the way you view yourself as a worker. Rarely, some piece of information will be so profound it may even disrupt the entire system. If you cannot assimilate the information according to your view of the world, then your view of the world will change.

Here are a few examples:

- You take a course on identifying birds and suddenly you are noticing and identifying birds you barely knew were there before.
- Someone points out you have a particular knack or skill, and you begin seeing ways to use your newly discovered talent.
- You learn that Eskimos have 16 words for snow and begin noticing that snow is not just snow.
- Your daughter announces that she is going to apply to a particular college, and you suddenly run into countless people who know about the school.
- You learn your company is going to downsize. Suddenly, your job security is shaken, and you notice everything about your workplace and the economy in general in vivid detail.

The list goes on. When you get a new piece of information, your life reorganizes around it. Obviously, some reorganization is more dramatic than others. Learning the names of birds will probably not have the same impact as discovering that you no longer want to or are able to pursue the career you have followed for 20 years.

Some information may totally dissipate your "career system," such as an injury or discovering the skills you have are no longer needed. The funnel below offers one explanation of how this change-of-view happens:

1. You find yourself without a job and wonder if you can network successfully. You don't think you have the confidence to express yourself. But you go to a meeting and find that you can explain your interests and your accomplishments.

The details of the meeti*ng* are not important.

2. You have learned that you can express yourself.

3. You now see yourself as someone who can network with others.

4. You will now look for networking opportunities with your newly found confidence.

Order Out of Chaos

While your career may seem to be governed more by chance than by design, the "funnel" tells us it may be more than just random chance. If you find something you like, it is because of "scanning and planning."

While building a system of beliefs about our careers, we continually adjust our four scans as we shape our career self-concept. As intentional beings, we can influence the way our four scans operate and the nature of our career self-concept as well as the way we live as productive individuals in the world.

The four scans screen the information we need to develop our sense of confidence as contributors and our self-esteem: Knowing what we can do and how well we do it. The information we scan also develops our sense of what matters to us in our work.

What we scan influences what we center our life around and the meaning our life holds for us. What we choose to see determines our sense of purpose by taking in information from our environment, gathering information, and synthesizing new ideas. Finally, we scan the information that helps us build, define, develop, and maintain productive relationships.

Now let's go to work on those four scans.

The First Scan: Building Momentum and Living Your Commitment to Your Future

"The last of the human freedoms is to choose one's attitudes." -- Victor Frankl

The first scan—scanning our willingness to build the momentum we need to keep moving toward success—refers to our level of self-confidence and how we see ourselves as someone who can get things done. If what we scan is essentially positive, we will gather positive and reassuring information. If we filter through only negative information, we find reasons to be discouraged.

Both the positive and the negative are there to pick from. Building momentum counts on making a commitment to scanning for positive information. Three dynamics influence the way we build this positive attitude:

1. *First, you believe the goals you set are worth the effort and that if you apply yourself you can succeed. If you think an opportunity to advance your career is beyond your ability, or if you are uncertain it is something you want, you will not expend much effort.*

2. *Second, you assume responsibility for the outcome of your efforts. Career development is not like buying a lottery ticket and hoping for the best. While finding opportunities may seem left to chance, you must make your own good luck by taking conscious and intentional action.*

3. *Third, you accept personal responsibility for your attitude and those intentional actions.*

Many people I have worked with are discouraged by the lack of personal satisfaction they had hoped to find in their careers. "Those who move ahead, however, do not let the absence of fulfillment trouble them. Individuals with confidence barely notice that they "tune" their scans to the positive. Their success is so ingrained that it becomes automatic. They subconsciously assume success, even when they experience the occasional failure.

At this point you may want to pause and go to the exercise in the back of this book, *Activity Three: Feelings Scale*

You can summarize these three dynamics that shape the first scan with the question, "What are you willing to do?" If you look for reasons why you might fail, you will find them. If you look for reasons why you might succeed, you will find these as well. We all hold a set of beliefs about our capacity to achieve goals and the level of responsibility we will take for our futures.

Momentum Building and Positive Attitude

Frankl sheds light on the role the success scan plays in our career success. Frankl was an inmate in a Nazi concentration camp during World War II. He endured and observed incredible suffering and left the experience with a profound understanding of human character. He observed that those who had a personal sense of mission, or a reason for living, survived. Those who did not, perished.

This feeling of mission, even optimism, is critical to building momentum. This does not imply the prisoners were happy with the way their lives were going at the time, but it does mean they knew they were part of something larger and more important than their current misfortune.

The active choice to embrace a positive attitude is indeed easy when things go well. When things are not going well, optimism takes practice. There will be times when you do not feel optimistic or in control. When that happens, learn to fake it.

During my limited theater experience, I learned a valuable lesson about momentum building from my college theater director, Minor Roots. He always admonished the cast and crew to say to anyone who asked that, "The play is going well," regardless of what was happening.

Describing your career progress is just like our college plays. The set may not be ready, the lights have been repossessed, and the lead player has laryngitis. But, overall, "The play is going well!"

If you want to be intentional about a career that self-organizes around your goals, consider that when things go well, you bask in success. When things are not turning out the way you would like, you endure and learn from the growth experience.

Another story: I was asked to present a mini-session on career planning to the inmates in a county jail. I found myself in the bowels of the facility and locked into a cinderblock room with stainless steel tables bolted to the floor.

My audience soon plodded in and sat around me, large and menacing. As I proceeded with my presentation, one inmate interrupted and announced that if he didn't get a job, he would take my money.

While his prison garb and the setting gave his threat some credibility, I pointed out that as soon as the inmate blamed others for not having a job, he had compromised his momentum. He was blaming others for his fate and not looking at what he could do for himself.

The inmate bought the concept and realized that stealing meant he believed that others had some power that he did not have. He was ready to go to work on his plan. Toward the end of the session, he described the pride he took in his skill as a machinist because he could do something that a lot of people could not do. He was ready to take responsibility for building momentum and scan positive information about his capacity to manage his career.

We all possess beliefs about our level of momentum regardless of our conscious thoughts. Frankl observed concentration camp inmates who viewed the situation as hopeless, and they simply decided to die. At the other extreme, he saw inmates who viewed their lives as having meaning so they were able to hang on. Ultimately, momentum building all comes down to facing that key question:

"What are you willing to do?"

At this point you might want to do Activity Four: Your "Go-for-It-Gauge"

The evidence to determine what you are willing to do is readily available. Your success patterns are already in place, and your experience can predict what you are willing to do.

I know that if I take conscious responsibility for my success, I will improve my chances of success markedly. I learned that at a young age. When I was in the sixth grade, the father of one of my friends took us to a nearby hill to ski. I decided to build a ski jump and climbed to the top of the hill to test my prowess as a ski jumper. I raced down the hill and promptly fell as I arrived at my jump.

After several repeats of this performance, my friend's father told me that he could see it in my face when I was going to fall. I was the saboteur of my own success.

In my heart, I realized I was afraid of the jump and planned to fall before ever going over the ramp. So I went back to the top, determined that the next time, if I fell, it would not be because I wanted to.

As you no doubt guessed, I raced down the hill and cleared the jump. My landing, however, was a disaster and I cartwheeled down the rest of the slope, thankful for the soft snow. I may have fallen anyway, but it was an honest fall, and the knowledge I gained led me to successful landings later that day. The secret:

Stop Trying!

The following twist of words may help you focus on the attitude you need to build the momentum you need in difficult situations. Imagine you are about to fly away to some distant destination. As you settle into your seat the pilot comes on the intercom:

*"Welcome to flight 357. We are now cleared for take-off. Please put your seatback trays in their upright position, fasten your seat belts, and I will **try** to fly the plane."*

"*Try"* is not what you want to hear from a pilot. Don't think about trying. Trying means you are willing to compromise your success. Focus on doing.

The Role of Superstition in Career Decision Making

Our capacity to recognize patterns depends on the filters we use to sort through the information that we continuously encounter. If the filters are not in place our heads would explode. You simply cannot take it all in, so filters are important. On the other hand, the filters we put into place count on our beliefs about where we have seen cause-and-effect relationships. If we refuse to walk under a ladder because we did it once and were struck on the head, avoiding ladders is a good thing. If we believe that walking under a ladder will control our destiny for the rest of the day, that's not so good. We may still want to go around the menace ladders present, but it might be wise to look up and see what's going on. We all have filters, or superstitions, which cause us to miss opportunities. If we are aware of the limits our filters can bring, we can be more open to monitoring our thoughts and behaviors.

You might like to review the list of suggestions in *Activity Five: Tips for momentum building*

The Second Scan: Knowing What Matters to You in the Work That You Do

"The unexamined life is not worth living." Socrates

Thinking back over your working life...

> When were the times that you jumped out of bed with enthusiasm and looked forward to the start of the day?
>
> When were you the most successful with things that you wanted to accomplish at work, at home, or even pursuing hobbies?
>
> On the other hand, when were the times you laid awake, worrying about something going on at work?

Keeping in mind that we see what we believe is important to us, answering those questions can help you understand what matters to you in your work. We want more of the positive work experiences and learn to avoid the negative ones. If we know our areas of enthusiasm and those things we would rather avoid, we will be more likely to spot opportunities.

To begin with, forget about job titles. Titles don't mean much. Look below the surface of job titles and job descriptions, and examine those skills, work environments, and work values that serve as the building blocks of the job.

Any system consists of the constant interaction of a handful of basic elements that build on themselves to create the complex structure of our work roles. Your job here is to understand your core work values, your core skills, and the work environments you prefer. Those elements are the building blocks of your ideal job. So the answer to the question, "What matters to you in the work that you do?" is not a job title.

Once you have a picture of the ideal, your serendipitous job search will become organized. You will also learn the sort of intuition that good career decision-making requires. The more you know, the more you will see. Let's start with temperament.

Scanning Your Temperament

Personal leadership requires reflection and a conscious effort to be as good at being you as you can be. Personal leadership means taking responsibility for becoming self-aware and using self-awareness to be better at being yourself.

The skills and characteristics we bring to work can be broken down into "above the waterline" behaviors and "below the waterline" behaviors. Like the iceberg with most of its mass below the water line, our most potent characteristics are hidden. It's our unique "below the water line" behavioral preferences that dictate our successes and failures.

"Above the water line behaviors" are traits that can be measured by resumes, job interviews, and references. This information tells a perspective employer if we have the skills to do the job. Our "below the water line behaviors" indicate if we will be able to get along with our colleagues, if we are reliable and dependable workers, or if we are inclined to steal. Those skills deal with temperament, emotional intelligence, motivation, integrity, and aptitude for learning.

Temperament came to light in the business and education communities thanks to the work of Isabel Myers and her mother Katherine Briggs and their work with Jungian type theory. You may have taken the Myers-Briggs Type Indicator (MBTI). If so, I suggest you review that material as it offers an excellent way to scan your preferences in the way you interact with your environment and with others. I will use the Big Five personality traits and the work of John Lounsbury and Lucy Gibson and their Personality Style Indicator. Those five aspects help us understand our preferences for interacting in the work place: agreeableness, conscientiousness, openness, emotional resilience, and extraversion.

As you progress through this section, there are several assumptions about temperament:

- Temperament refers to personality traits, such as openness or extroversion.
- They are innate rather than learned.
- Temperament influences our learned behavior.
- Temperament can be measured.

Our unique combination of these five personality qualities can be brought to bear on our business problems with great efficiency. Scanning your temperament helps you understand the drivers behind your work behaviors, particularly decision making. We can access the "below the waterline" characteristics that influence career success.

At this point you may want go to the exercise in the back of this book, *Activity Six:* Tuning your Scanner with an Awareness of Your Temperament Preferences

Agreeableness: Individuals who are highly agreeable appear compassionate and cooperative. Those less agreeable may seem to lack trust and confidence in their colleagues. The latter will assert that they know their business and won't get swayed just to go along with the group. Highly agreeable people want everyone to get along, even when they're wrong. We all have to get along with others at least part of the time to get by. These others include co-workers, bosses, customers we don't really like, and people who make us angry or insult us. Lucy Gibson, vice president at Resource Associates, points out that it takes time and effort to develop relationships that bring us joy.

Agreeable people tend to:

- Be accommodating and tolerant
- Display behaviors that support a sense of harmony and community in the work group
- Avoid discussions that would lead to animosity or hurt feelings

Less agreeable people:

- Express strong opinions
- Are willing to disagree
- Stick to their beliefs rather than go with the group

To tap into the level of agreeableness you bring to your work, you might describe a time when your views conflicted with the group. How did you handle it? When you believed others on your team were taking a wrong approach, how did you approach them? Answering these questions may help you adjust any of your behaviors, if need be.

Conscientiousness: Conscientiousness defines a preference for planning or a preference for spontaneity. Do you prefer the symphony (highly structured) or New Orleans jazz (relies on spontaneity)? We all learn a tremendously long list of rules. Some rules we obey scrupulously; others we fudge. Some people bend the rules more than others.

Conscientiousness does not necessarily equate to honesty or integrity. I worked with managers at a large plant that employed many complex techniques from science and engineering. The managers appeared to be far from conscientious, yet the company was very profitable. They told me they made their decisions based on the principles of engineering, not on what their bosses always wanted them to do. Managers need to set up a workplace that reinforces rule adherence and honesty without squelching imagination and creativity.

Conscientious individuals are:

- Dependable and accept the importance of rules

- Tend to take a fairly rigid approach to organizational policies

- Always respectful of authority and the company hierarchy

People who may not be seen as conscientious tend to:
- Personalize the rules

- Prefer using their own judgment over taking direction from authority

- Do well with planning and development tasks

For a personal scan, describe a time when you took a shortcut or bypassed some steps at work to get something done quicker, better, or more efficiently. Did you find it productive to sidestep the rules, or more productive to stay within the rules? How could the organizations you worked for have reduced the bureaucracy or red tape to help you be more effective?

Openness: Openness speaks to an interest in adventure and curiosity. The lack of openness implies some discomfort with change and an attitude of caution. Workers need some degree of open-mindedness or they set themselves up as a Luddite very quickly. On the other hand, some discretion is needed so that they don't pursue every whim. Technology offers some an opportunity to become distracted by every new gadget, while those who are closed may miss opportunities to take advantage of new ideas.

The trick comes when we try to find the sweet spot on the openness spectrum. How do we remain open enough to take advantage of innovation and remain agile, while not finding ourselves chasing after every new and unusual shiny object? Generally, one person will struggle to find the "sweet spot," leaving us to rely on teamwork as the route for finding the best balance between innovation and stability.

Less open individuals:

- Prefer predictable, procedure-based jobs
- Prefer not to move into different areas or participate in training programs
- Prefer co-workers who are very similar to themselves
- Might complain if goals keep changing

More open individuals:

- Enjoy some change, variety, and novelty in the job
- Like to learn new things
- Adapt well to technological and organizational change
- Are more accepting of cultural diversity
- Might encourage the group to be open to new ideas

In order to understand your preference, consider a time when a past employer underwent a major change. How did you react? If you were asked how your company can change to improve productivity, did you see change as disruptive and threatening, or, at the other extreme, chase after change for the sake of change?

Emotional Resilience: Emotional resilience or flexibility describes the range of responses encountered in a business or educational setting. This scale helps us understand how we can be empathetic toward others without becoming so anxious about the feelings of others that we can't make good business decisions. George Washington wrote his brother saying, "I heard the bullets whistle, and, believe me, there is something charming in the sound." That attitude toward being in battle may represent a certain emotional resilience as compared to those of us who jump at the sound of a loud noise.

One could argue that George's resilience might not always be healthy. Successful display of emotional resilience means we react appropriately to a stressful situation. It may mean pausing before we speak, speaking up immediately, or running as fast as we can for safety. The context dictates what is appropriate. Lashing out in anger when we are confronted or cowering in the face of bullies may be seen as lacking emotional resilience. Extreme resilience may make us seem aloof or uncaring, while a lack of emotional resilience could leave us a wet mess at the slightest provocation, making us unreliable. Those who are emotionally resilient can do what they need to do regardless of their emotional state. Developing emotional resilience keeps us from letting stress interfere with our effectiveness.

Less emotionally resilient individuals:

- May be emotionally reactive in most situations
- Find themselves overly sensitive to external events
- Depend on the positive regard of others to maintain their self-esteem

Emotionally resilient individuals

- Tend to remain calm a during crises
- Seem level-headed to others

- Are able to handle personal responsibilities
- Do not let external events bother them

No work setting is free from stress, and conflict is expected from time to time. Scan a time when you handled conflict well and a time when you did not handle it well, and imagine how you might have faced a situation with greater emotional resilience. That may give you some insight into your emotional resilience.

Extroversion

Like the other scales, this is a spectrum without absolutes. Your place on extroversion/introversion scale depends on your source of stimulation. If it tends to come from solitary activity, you lean toward the introverted end of the spectrum. If you draw your energy from the interaction with others, you lean toward the extroverted end of the scale. Few people dwell on either extreme. I, for example, speak in public a great deal and I am continually going to meetings and gatherings where I interact with people I don't know. These sorts of activities would suggest I am an extrovert. Once these meetings are over, however, I want to crawl into my cave and be left alone, the hallmark of a committed introvert. Introversion has little to do with being shy or withdrawn, any more than extroverts are driven to be the life of the party with every breath they take.

Less extroverted individuals:

- Tend to be quiet, low-key, deliberate, and less involved in the social world.
- Need less stimulation than other people and more time alone.
- Prefer working by themselves

Extroverted individuals

- Seek out stimulation and the company of others.
- Are usually enthusiastic and action-oriented.
- Enjoy being with people and participating in social gatherings.

Motivation

Remember Tom Sawyer and the fence that needed to be whitewashed? An external influence or motivator, his Aunt Polly, and the slipper she used to spank him with, motivated Tom to paint the fence. He did not want the job at all and preferred other entertainment.

He pretended, however, that he was doing a great, enjoyable thing to persuade other children to do the job for him. The victims of his swindle thought they were doing a very adult thing and having fun. Fun is an internal motivator. Internal forces drove them.

As Mark Twain wrote:

"If he (Tom Sawyer) had been a great and wise philosopher, he would now have comprehended that work consists of whatever a body is obliged to do, and that play consists of whatever a body is not obliged to do."

Consider the external and internal motivators you need in order to work on a particular project. All of them need to be in place if you are to excel.

External factors that need to be in place or you will face dissatisfaction:

What role does the nature of the company have on your work behaviors? One of my clients loved his job except for the fact that his company sold tobacco. Dissatisfaction with his perception of the morality of the product led him to want to leave.

What are your expectations concerning company policy and administration? One company I observed had severe morale problems due to the way it made decisions and showed favoritism. Sadly, the company's leadership was not aware of the effect of their policies and could not understand the large turnover in employees.

How do you prefer to be supervised? Most of the managers, technicians, and engineers I work with favor autonomy and teamwork rather than close supervision. Others prefer straightforward direction and then being left alone to do the job.

Which working conditions do you prefer? Obvious differences are indoor or outdoor occupations. Working conditions are a more complicated matter. One of my clients took a retail job while he waited to return to his job as a quality control chemist in a manufacturing plant. He confessed that waiting on customers was very uncomfortable. He described himself as a "mill rat," knowing production work was his preferred environment.

What role do interpersonal relations play in your job? I offered to do a workshop on interpersonal relations at a residential care center. The nurses were quite excited at the prospect of learning more about each other. One maintenance supervisor wanted to know, however, "why we can't just come to work, do our jobs, and go home." He saw interpersonal relationships on the job in a much different manner than his colleagues.

What do you expect from your salary? Our relationship with money is complex since money symbolizes different things to different people. What the money may buy is certainly attractive, but money itself does not generally inspire excellence for long. At one university, the faculty was not particularly well paid, yet they were all highly motivated and worked hard. When the board of regents cut their salaries five percent, morale plummeted. The formerly motivated, if underpaid, faculty became extremely dissatisfied despite the fact that not much had really changed about their financial situation.

Does status matter to you? No one I know wants to be taken for granted, and if we are, we quickly become disgruntled. The favored parking place, the corner office, the larger cubicle—these may all be tokens of status. Does recognition, such as status symbols like the corner office, move you from "disgruntled" back to "gruntled?"

How important is job security? If you are an entrepreneur or a consultant, your security needs are lower than someone who does not like risk. If job security is important, you will be willing to forgo autonomy and higher earnings in favor of confidence in regular earnings. If you prefer security, you would never work on commission.

Internal factors that help you excel on the job:

1. **How do feelings of achievement influence your performance?** Achievement could come from seeing the immediate results of your work, as a sculptor or dental hygienist might. Others may get a feeling of achievement from knowing they have done all they could in accord with their professional standards, such as a teacher or religious leader. Writing this book does both for me: I draw a sense of achievement from seeing the completed text and knowing that I have given people helpful material.

2. **Are you motivated by recognition?**
Recognition may be very public or simply an occasional informal or private comment. It might take a form you do not expect. In my salad days, I wrote songs and performed them

in smoke-filled bars while earning money for graduate school. I was socializing with some friends on a night I wasn't performing and heard another singer perform one of my songs. I was pleasantly astounded, very flattered, and insufferable for some time afterwards. (I'm obviously still bragging about it.) Medals and awards tend to be less motivating than more immediate feedback.

3. **What does growth and advancement mean to you?**
At one point in the development of our economy, we were supposed to scramble up the corporate ladder. With the huge discrepancy between upper management salary and workers' wages, the climb may still be appealing, but with the decline in the number of middle level managers and the advent of team management, the ladder shrinks. Furthermore, many of those in management come from liberal arts backgrounds. Engineers and related technical professionals prefer to use their technical knowledge. As a result, a large number of professionals do not require much supervision management, yet still long to be moving up to something. For some of us, the corporate ladder is still appealing, but for most, I think growth means more knowledge in our field and autonomy as members of a small business, or the opportunity to pursue projects that appeal to us.

4. **How interested are you in the job that you do?**
Refer back to Tom Sawyer and the fence. What entices you to do the work that you do? If you do not like what you are doing now, what would have to change to make it interesting to you?

As you look at the items below, consider that you do not need to know how they motivate you, just understand how they matter to you in the work that you do.

Work Factors

Company policies and practices: What is a minimum that you would consider? Are there particular personnel practices you expect? Do you prefer a loosely structured work environment or one with clearly defined rules?

Salary and benefits: Would you work on commission? What is the minimum level of benefits you expect? What salary do your skills and experience command? What sort of life style do you intend to support?

Respect: How do you expect to be treated by supervisors and by peers?

Safety: What level of risk will you accept on the job or commuting to your job?

Relationship with peers: Do you prefer to work in teams or alone?

Working conditions: Work environments vary considerably, and they are influenced by many conditions. What is the range of conditions you find acceptable?

Status: How much responsibility do you intend to assume? Do public perceptions of your job matter to you?

Quality of supervision: What sort of relationship do you expect to have with supervisors, assuming you have any supervisors?

Relations with subordinates: If people report to you, how do you expect those relationships to be structured?

Creativity needs: What does creativity mean to you and how much do you need in your work?

Intellectual stimulation: Are you motivated by ideas for their own sake? Do you find yourself attracted to learning and problem solving?

Satisfaction from work being done: Does the work itself bring you personal satisfaction?

Autonomy: Do you prefer to succeed or fail based upon your own merits?

Collegial/collaborative relationships: Does the opportunity to work on a team attract you?

Achievement needs: Do you need to tackle difficult tasks and to overcome all obstacles?

Personality Style

John Holland developed a model to assist career decision-making based on the idea that certain personalities gravitate toward certain environments.
You might want to visit a career professional to take an interest inventory such as the Self-Directed Search, published by PAR; the Strong, published by Consulting Psychologist Press; or the Career Decision Making System, published by Pearson's Clinical Assessment group. They are usually available for a modest fee.

Below I have identified the Holland types with a brief description and some key adjectives that describe people who fall into one of the types. Reviewing this list will help you develop a vocabulary to describe your strengths.

It is not so important that you find which of the six or combination of the six personality types you fit into. I hope you will come away with a better understanding of what matters to you in the work place, which will help you tune your scanner and identify your ideal work settings.

1. Read through each brief example.
2. Highlight the area or areas that sound like you.
3. Underline the adjectives that describe you.
4. Complete the form at the end of the list to help organize and reflect on what you have learned. That helps build intuition to tune your scanner and help organize serendipity.

I have used the personality-type definitions from both the Self-Directed Search and the Career Decision Making System in the event that you use an interest inventory in conjunction with this exercise.

> **Realistic or Crafts:** You prefer hands-on activities and one-on-one discussions rather than group talks. You like to try things first and then decide whether you like it or not.

You also like to know exactly how a process is going to work before you jump in.

Terms that might describe you: Athletic, conforming, frank, honest, humble, materialistic, mechanical, modest, natural, outdoor type, persistent, practical, realistic, rugged, self-reliant, shy, stable, strong, technical, thrifty.

Investigative or Scientific: You like to be very thorough with the things that you do, and you prefer to take a methodical, problem-solving approach. You also like research as well as analyzing yourself and your background. You might avoid risk-taking and prefer to be cautious and conservative when trying new things.

Terms that might describe you: Analytical, cautious, creative, critical, curious, independent, intellectual, introverted, logical, mathematical, methodical, modest, precise, questioning, rational, reserved, scientific, studious.

Artistic: You like spontaneity and prefer less structure than other types, such as clerical. You may have some ideas about your dream job. You like being creative rather than systematic, and you would rather let your work flow than stick to deadlines and a schedule.

Terms that might describe you: Artistic, creative, complicated, disorderly, emotional, expressive, idealistic, imaginative, impractical, impulsive, independent, innovative, insightful, intuitive, non-conforming, original, perceptive, reflective, sensitive.

Social: You like to talk, and you seek environments that are open and supportive. Your positive experiences generally involve other people, and you like being part of social groups.

Terms that might describe you: Accepting, altruistic, caring, convincing, cooperative, empathetic, friendly, generous, helpful, humanitarian, idealistic, insightful, kind, persuasive, responsible, sociable, tactful, understanding.

Enterprising or Business: You enjoy being challenged and prefer thought-provoking experiences with lots of verbal interaction. You would rather talk than write or listen. You are also achievement-oriented and would rather do than analyze. You may be impulsive at times and prefer action to planning.

Terms that might describe you: Acquisitive, adventurous, ambitious, attention-getting, articulate, assertive, confident, determined, dominant, domineering, energetic, enthusiastic, flirtatious, impulsive, influential, optimistic, persuasive, pleasure-seeking, political, popular, productive, resourceful, self-confident, sociable.

Conventional or Clerical: You enjoy structure and want to know exactly what will happen to you. Your decision-making is highly structured.

Terms that might describe you: Conforming, conscientious, calm, careful, conservative, conventional, dependable, efficient, inhibited, methodical, obedient, orderly, organized, persistent, practical, reliable, systematic, traditional, unimaginative, well-controlled.

Now go back through your checkmarks and pick the five adjectives that you believe describe you best. Copy the following table onto another piece of paper and use the table to personalize what the terms mean for you.

Term	*Sociable*
Example	*I get along easily with others*
How it can help you	*Team building,*

	motivation, pleasant work place
How it can get in your way	*Visit and socialize with people; may emphasize relationships over tasks*
Workplace expectations for you	*I like working with others but also need time to work alone*
Workplace expectations for employers	*See me as a leader and team member but also be careful I am not distraction at times*
Marketing points	*My leadership and motivation experiences*
Marketing example	*Use of portfolios to evaluate leadership performance*
Leadership/ supervision needs	*Want to be a decision maker but also enjoy a team environment*
Environment needs	*Social contact*

At this point, you may want to consider completing the exercises *Activity Seven: Tuning Your Scanner with a Career Experience Timeline* and *Activity Eight: Tuning Your Scanner with Your Ideal Job Description*

Your Ideal job description

With these thoughts about what matters to you in mind, let's focus on them a bit. Most job titles come with a job description that may or may not match the way the job is actually practiced. You were attracted to the job because you believed it offered something, or once you were in, you shaped the job to your desires.

This activity actually works in reverse. Here you will describe the elements of the job without worrying about what the job is called. Will you find this ideal? Probably you will not. But you will improve your chances of coming close to your ideal once you focus on what you are seeking in it. Your scanner will be tuned, and your intuition will be in overdrive.

First: Describe the job's mission. What difference does the job make? What does it produce or what service does it provide?

Second: What skills are involved? What does someone need to know to occupy this position? How do they usually spend their day?

Third: What is the reporting structure? Who does someone in this position report to, and who reports to him or her?

Organizing your thoughts around these questions will narrow your focus and increase your chances of finding positions that fit your ideal.

At this point you might want to complete **Activity Nine: Your Thirty-Second Commercial**

Summary

Knowing what matters to you in the work you do helps you spot opportunities. If you don't know what you are looking for, you probably won't find it. Clarifying what gets you out of bed in the morning and eager to go to work helps draw you to those serendipitous contacts that lead to career growth and satisfaction. Remember, there are no coincidences.

The Third Scan: Intentional Learning And Synthesis

"Our security and prosperity will grow out of our ability to effectively master a process of continually creating new solutions."
David Kahle

The third scan addresses the way you handle three tasks:

- Gathering new information
- Personalizing the information
- Applying what you learn toward reaching your goals

It's all about changing your behavior on the basis of new learning. We are all naturally creative, always developing new concepts to help us understand the world around us. As self-organizing systems who continuously adapt to the world around us, we gather new information and form new opinions on how to apply our new learning.

Learning here refers to gathering the knowledge we need to continue to re-create ourselves and remain agile in the work place. Information comes from four sources:

1. Experiential learning
2. Formal learning
3. Self-directed informal learning
4. Knowledge we create from other sources

Your beliefs about your career are the creation of all that you have learned. What you have learned in the past controls your career behaviors now.

For everything you do that is effective, and for everything you do that is not effective, you learn. You will cling tenaciously to all those behaviors that work. This is a good thing. You will also cling with equal tenacity and determination to all that does not work. It is challenging to know the difference and then take action.

As an intentional learner, you try to maintain enough regularity in the information you gather so you can not only function effectively, but also create enough irregularity to notice discrepancies between what you believe and what you see. Learning and creativity live on the chaotic edge of our normally systematic lives.

So look in odd places for information and challenge yourself in new ways as part of your intentional learning efforts.

Learning begins when we know what it is that we don't know:

- *Experiential: "What was that noise?"*

- *Formal: "If I want that promotion, I better take that course in cost-accounting."*

- *Self-directed: "I can't figure out how to work this machine. Where are the directions?"*

- *New knowledge: "We have seen this problem before. Now we need to come up with some preventive solutions."*

The Level of Intentionality and Learning

We gather information from any number of places, some intentional and some not so intentional. In intentional learning, we attend to all learning experiences and do not discount learning from informal sources. It is easy to imagine a classroom when we think of "intentional" learning.

Certainly, formal programs are one source but not the most common source of learning. The four areas mentioned above and described below offer several ways to look at sources of information and tune our scanners to multiple learning opportunities.

Experiential learning is at the bottom of the pyramid because we can approach experiential learning passively. We do not have to do anything; it just happens. Formal learning can be passive as well. External sources, usually teachers and textbooks, organize our learning and often fill us like empty jugs. Self-directed learning is harder because we are both teacher and pupil. Synthesis is hardest of all because we invent what we are learning.

Experiential Learning

We constantly create knowledge from experience. Every waking moment is crowded with experiential learning. The primary way we make sense of this onslaught of data is bias.

We use bias to shape our scanner to screen what we choose to accept to believe and help dictate our actions. The challenge is to understand how our bias operates on our information receptors. We can think about bias with the help of the four scans:

- If we have confidence, we can succeed in the face of a given task. If we believe the reward is worth the effort, we will invest more energy in trying to understand any experiences than if we harbor self-doubt or question the worth of what we see before us.

- If the experience connects on some level with what we believe interests us, then we will be open to learning.

- If the experience calls upon our use of learning methods that are comfortable, we are more likely to pursue the information. We are also more likely to notice information that is near at hand rather than seek new sources of information.

- If information concerns relationships that we believe are in our self-interest to pursue, we are more likely to involve ourselves in them.

Our challenge as intentional learners is to recognize the information we filter out and make a conscious decision to either continue to filter it out or go beyond our comfort level and consider new information. Once intentional filtering begins, learning becomes more self-directed.

Formal Learning

Formal learning occurs when we follow a curriculum set by someone else. Workshops and college courses are examples of formal learning. Formal learning also includes programs sponsored by your employer. It comes second on the intentional learning pyramid because we can easily take on learning prescribed by others without much personal intention to do so. When we take responsibility for our success in a formal learning setting, we approach a level of self-directed learning. For example, if we prepare for a class by mastering the topic beforehand, we have raised our level of commitment and our level of mastery.

Self-Directed, Informal Learning

The difference between experiential learning and self-directed learning is one of intention. Experiential learning comes from casual experience. We move up to self-directed learning when we seek to create our learning experiences. Self-directed learning occurs when you are motivated to seek out information and you take action. When you are curious about something, such as a sudden noise or something you hear on the evening news and launch your personal investigation, you become a self-directed learner. In the workplace this generally refers to the research you might do to solve a problem. You have a question such as "How does the machine work?" or "What do I need to know about that company before I do business with them?"

Self-directed learning at its best occurs when we set learning objectives and then design a course of study. One readily accessible source of self-directed learning is simply reading the directions (a great career boost, by the way). These "mini-courses" can go from acquiring information on an immediate issue to pursuing a life-long interest on some topic that interests us. Many of us apply self-directed learning to hobbies such as learning about compost, the perfect golf swing, or a craft skill, say ceramics. In fact, you are probably already a good self-directed learner.

Synthesis

Synthesis is the effort to create new ideas from experience and new learning. Synthesis helps us reshape the way we conduct our careers and offer new ideas for the workplace. All of our other learning leads to synthesis. For example, if we take a formal course in a new accounting method, we can apply that method to our work setting. We have synthesized new information. Since things seldom are a perfect fit, we need to invent new knowledge for the new accounting method to work.

How Do You Prefer to Learn?

Several attempts have been made to organize learning styles through such activities as the Herman Brain Dominance Inventory and the Gregorc Style Delineator. The following categories encourage you to build your capacity to learn in areas where are you are not so confident. You are not likely to find any one category completely suited to you. Borrow from each of the four to identify your unique style.

Analyzers: These people like to simplify and examine things. They enjoy thinking about new ideas and talking about them in a logical way. They also rely on logic to approach things and appreciate attention to detail, but find they have little time for it. Analyzers can become impatient with people who don't think and reason the way they do. People who analyze often think that people who visualize their goals are too unfocused.

Analyzers use logical thinking to research ideas, create new products, find solutions to difficult problems, and develop new theories. Extremely strong analyzers tend to dislike detail-oriented meetings, reporting to others, and doing unnecessary paperwork. They often become impatient with people who rely on feelings more than analytic skills.

The Analyzer's Preferred Learning Style: Classroom instruction as well as individual and team research. Analyzers lean toward the theoretical and can learn for learning's sake without necessarily seeing the practical results. They can be very good at designing their own learning and often subscribe to magazines such as *Scientific American*.

Visualizers: These people like to picture things in their mind. They think about people and objects in terms of visual images and metaphors. They also like to look ahead and see the possibilities. Visualizers often have difficulty paying attention to one subject for very long and tend to work in bursts of energy, moving quickly from one project to another. They may also have difficulty communicating with others because their "picture of things" is hard to put into words. They are impatient with time spent on analysis or details.

In addition, visualizers like being artistic and using personal expression and creativity. They visualize and discuss future possibilities or new ways to interpret old ideas. They enjoy and seek out change. Extremely strong visualizers like to have their ideas accepted, but often resist explaining their picture of things in detail for others. They risk being misunderstood by others because their visions or ideas can be unfocused or too personal.

The Visualizer's Preferred Learning Style: Classroom and group discussion. Visualizers enjoy working on the theoretical and can be impatient when sharing learning, especially with other learning styles such as connectors and organizers. Learning is fun for this group. They subscribe to *National Geographic* and watch a lot of Public Broadcasting as well as the History Channel.

Organizers: People who use this style like to keep busy any way they can—building, making, fixing, playing, and exercising—and they like to see the results of their efforts. They are comfortable with structure and work well when things are well-organized. Their preference is to have someone else worry about "the big picture" while they sort out and work on the finer details. They like to complete one project before they move on to another and enjoy being active while often thinking of people who spend their time analyzing, connecting, or visualizing as too inactive or as wasting time.

Persons preferring this style tend to seek hands-on work that produces practical goods or services. They enjoy mastering the fine details of a job and prefer predictable schedules. They also liked work tasks and jobs with clear-cut beginnings and endings. Extremely strong organizers like to know exactly what is expected of them on the job. They get impatient with persons who do not appreciate the need for attention to detail.

The Organizer's Preferred Learning Style: Organizers want to know the immediate purpose of their learning and do not want to learn the theory; they just want to do the work. *"I don't care how it works; just tell me which button to push."* Organizers do not care for the classroom setting unless it is immediately "hands on." They do not do well in group discussions but prefer to get right to work. They learn best with clear direction and with help outlining the details and the process as opposed to viewing the big picture and being left to fill in the blanks.

Connectors: People who use this style rely on their feelings. When they talk with others, they believe what is being felt is more important than what is being said. They like to connect to others with feelings and ideals, to seek harmony, and be supportive of others. Often, they are labeled as sentimental. Because they rely on feelings more than words, connectors often have difficulty telling others what they mean; they view analyzing thoughts and actions as cold and impersonal.

Connectors are also drawn to jobs that help or serve others. They enjoy working with people or being around others while they work. Extremely strong connectors need to feel they are accomplishing something through their efforts and that they are appreciated. They often get impatient with others who apparently lack an understanding of feelings and human needs.

The Connector's Preferred Learning Style: Connectors enjoy group learning projects. Once the topic is presented, they want to talk about it. They do well in study circles and shared learning. They can also thrive in a classroom setting, especially if the class is small, and if they have frequent contact with the instructor and fellow learners. They may need reassurance for their learning goals and their progress.

Summary: The Intentional Learning Plan

The intentional learning plan is one way to review your thinking about intentional learning. You can use this format as your intentional learning contract, but it is primarily intended here as a prompt to help you think how you can use the preceding material in your current and future work roles.

Addressing each of the following areas helps you tune your scanner to your learning needs and your employer's learning needs, and reach your learning goals:

1. State the business need you are targeting in your learning plan.

2. What is the area you want to work on?

3. What do you intend to learn to resolve this stated business need?

4. What do you expect to happen as a result of your plan of action?

5. What other skills do you intend to acquire that are not directly related to the identified issue above?

6. How will your plan of action enrich...

   - You?
   - Your internal customers?
   - Your external customers?
   - The overall company?

7. What existing resources will you leverage to support your plan?

8. What solutions will you provide for the identified issue?

9. How will you measure your plan's success?

The Fourth Scan: Building Synergistic Relationships by Reaching Out to the World with All You Have to Offer

Grant that I may not so much seek to be understood as to understand.
Taken from a prayer attributed to St. Francis of Assisi

This chapter—covering the last of the four scans—shows how the power of our careers comes from our capacity to build relationships, manage our learning, while remaining optimistic. The quote above could be taken from anything from Zoroastrian philosophy to The Seven Habits of Highly Effective People. Building synergistic relationships depends on our ability to understand others and communicate that understanding back to them.

Our career self-concepts are created through our interactions with others. Our success in life depends on developing interdependent relationships. This ability begins with networking—showing that understanding others before you seek to have them understand you help develop such relationships.

We will explore a paradigm shift away from the idea that you are searching for jobs to the belief that you are searching for opportunities to solve problems for others. Regardless of your profession, you make a positive difference in the lives of those around you.

No matter the occupation, you are helping others. I was presenting a workshop to a group of adult educators some time ago, and one of the participants and I were walking to the lunchroom when we encountered a janitor vacuuming the lounge. He shut off the vacuum, pulled it out of our way, smiled, and said "Hello."

We acknowledged his greeting and went on our way. My companion remarked, "If we had reached him with our program, he would not have to be a janitor." But if my companion had read this book, he would realize that there are no drudgery jobs, just drudgery attitudes.

I do not want to eat my meals in dirty restaurants. When I am on the road, a courteous wait staff makes for a true, qualitative difference in my travel experience. If I have a good travel experience, the work I do helping people with career development issues is certainly a lot easier. This book centers on the janitor's reasons for offering the services he offers and the synergy he forms with those he services.

What I want to teach in this chapter is that you can use your knowledge of the problems you want to solve and offer your favorite abilities to help others. Not all of us can practice the selfless dedication of a Mother Teresa, but we can practice a commitment to improving any situation we encounter.

I call it "platform plus." That means knowing the standards that are expected and then imagining one more thing to go beyond what people expect. You can surprise people with service that exceeds.

Your marketing plan is based on a search for synergy. Synergy occurs when two entities come together to form a third entity greater than the sum of what the original entities can offer by themselves. In other words, if someone hires you, how will they be better off than they were before you arrived? Your marketing plan is based on the desire and evidence that you can answer those three questions.

When we combine an ethic of service with the basic reasons that any job exists, we create a marketing process that allows us to build synergy. You know what you want to do, and you know what matters to you in the work you do. Now you need to present the sorts of problems you want to solve in light of what your prospective client/employer needs and wants.

For example, look at this want ad adapted from *The Wall Street Journal*:

Senior HR Management Opportunities

Dynamic Southwestern Merchant Energy Company needs strategic thinkers to join its management team. Be a member of this collaborative HR team. We are currently recruiting for the following positions:

<u>DIRECTOR, HR OPERATIONS</u>

Directs all aspects of human resource operations for a diverse corporation in a rapidly-changing industry. Provides leadership for HR functional areas, including anticipating trends and developing programs supporting business strategy. Manages the administration and oversight of all labor relations programs and policies, including contract negotiation and administration. Collaborates with the HR team on performance management and other HR initiatives.

QUALIFICATIONS:
Strong experience and training in HR disciplines with solid business experience in a team-oriented environment. Demonstrated accomplishments in all areas of labor relations. Practical experience turning theory into outcomes supporting business strategy. Minimum 10 years of experience in HR. Bachelor's degree required; Master's degree preferred.

First and foremost, is this a job that you want? You do not want to apply for what you can do; you want to apply for what you <u>want</u> to do!

Once your target looks appealing to you, you can focus on understanding the needs and wants of your future client/employer. How does the HR director solve problems that the company needs solved? Are the HR issues that are unique to the company? Clearly, he or she can be involved with managing compensation and benefits; training and career development; employee relations and discipline; staffing, recruiting, hiring and firing; and developing employee policies and procedures.

In any of those roles, the director must see that the company is staffed with employees the company can afford (save money), that its policies meet the employees' fundamental expectations for fair treatment (save even more money), and that the company does not get sued for some perceived labor law infraction by a disgruntled employee (save a lot of money). The role of saving money in this manner can become invisible to other managers unless the HR staff blunders.

If successful, HR may not be noticed at all. Knowing these needs will be fundamental. You should mine your experience for evidence that you can do all these things and are able to offer the facts and figures to prove it.

All of these issues come under "Directs all aspects of human resource operations for a diverse corporation in a rapidly-changing industry." This is the foundation and may not actually come up in the discussion with the hiring manager.

If we look at the advertisement, other key terms appear: "Experience in a team-oriented environment" and "turn theory into outcomes supporting business strategy" may be fluff or might hint at the need for visionary leadership. In the heading, the advertisement calls for "strategic thinkers." Now we come to the art of marketing your talents. What are the real problems that the company running this ad needs to solve?

Every Job Exists Because of Some Business Problem That Needs Solving

Beyond the normal functions expected in the advertised HR position, the hiring managers have something on their minds. There is some issue they are either excited about or that worries them. This passion or pain will not be in the ad.

You thus need to find out what is behind their recruitment effort. Simply put, what are the gaps between where they are now and where they want to be, and how will the new HR manager fill the gap? They no doubt need someone to fill the gap created by growth or departure of the incumbent manager, but there is more to it than that. You can count on it.

The Passion and the Pain

At the heart of the position is the role it plays in completing the company's mission. Judging by the heading on the ad, it has something to do with selling energy. So anything you can learn about opportunities for that industry in the Southwest will help you market your skills.

More specifically, what are the human resource issues in that area for energy companies? They may not be readily apparent, but you can be sure that managers have them very much on their minds.

As to the "passion" end of the spectrum, staff members may have projects in mind that excite them and that they want HR to support. The HR department may be involved in a new initiative and hopes to see that effort bloom under new leadership.

On the "pain" end of the spectrum, the company leadership may have problems with HR they hope to resolve. If you can discover that concern, you can gather the experiences from your background that documents your ability to support their passions and relieve their pain.

Simply put, discover these key perspectives of the person who is hiring:

- What excites them?
- What worries them?

Where to Look

In all probability, you are no more than three networking contacts away from someone who can tell you all you need to know. The contact stream may start anywhere. In my search experiences, I heard about jobs through many sources:

- A family friend
- An ad on the bulletin board in the college placement office
- Participating in a college internship
- Calling on representatives of the industry
- Talking with a guitar player in a bar
- A college professor in graduate school
- A casual conversation in an automobile repair shop
- A conversation with a consultant

- From one of my students
- Overhearing a comment about a special project during a tour of an educational facility, and then making inquiries
- A conversation with a vendor
- Keeping up with blogs on LinkedIn
- Perusing web sites

Anyone reading this book can generate a similar list of the odd places they have heard about job leads. Keeping the scanner tuned and continuing to focus in on odd places is the best way to take advantage of these seemingly serendipitous opportunities.

As I thought about what I had done to gather information about passion and pain in the workplace, I discovered an equally odd and varied list:

- People I already knew
    - Neighbors
    - Friends
    - Relatives
    - Colleagues
    - Members of civic and church groups
    - My vendors
    - My customers
    - Attendees at various meetings:
        - Chamber gatherings
        - Social events
        - Conferences
        - Classes
        - Seminars
        - Professional groups
    - Barbers and hairstylists
    - Government workers
    - People in line with me at grocery stores and other retail outlets

- People I sought out:
    - Competitors of the business I was courting

- Customers of the business I was courting
- Suppliers for the business I was courting
- People who worked for the company I was courting
- People who lived in the town of the company I was pursuing

- And on line
  - Emailing my contact list
  - Posting on LinkedIn
  - Joining LinkedIn groups
  - Researching companies and individuals' LinkedIn pages, Facebook pages, and websites
  - Seeking out blogs and joining in the conversation

Another approach: If they have a pulse, network!

If they know one other person, they can help you. Throughout networking, one rule always applies: Keep doing it. If you are mixing two substances in order to form a compound, you know from basic chemistry that the more you stir, the more likely the molecules will bump into each other and bond.

The more you network, the more likely you are to run into opportunities. Given that you are three contacts away from all the information you need, and that the stream through those three contacts could start anywhere, you should network widely and often.

If I wanted to pursue the HR position in the advertisement, I would do several things. First, the ad appears to be offered through a placement agency or recruiter, otherwise known as a headhunter. To get the name of the company, you can do a fishing expedition of the area, or you can contact the headhunter and express your interest.

Follow one path or the other. Do not do both. If you look on your own first, once you express your interest, the recruiter is out of the picture. While that may benefit the hiring company (they won't have to pay the recruiter's fee), they also may prefer to let the recruiter filter candidates for them.

It is crucial that you understand this scanning process. If you are not a strong match for the position, but still believe you can help, you do not want to talk to the recruiter or HR. Their job is to limit the amount of applicants to the exact matches, and that may leave you out of the running. You want to get your story in front of the hiring manager. While you are seeking out the decision maker, HR is going to work diligently to filter the contacts and disruptions their managers might encounter from job seekers.

Now for a show of hands: *How many of you would rather take a beating then go to a meeting where you don't know anybody?* We are fundamentally tribal creatures comfortable with those we know and resistant to those we do not know. That desire to be with those familiar to us comes with being human. I worked with one very intelligent and capable individual who would rather be set on fire than meet a group of strangers. I convinced him to attend a meeting of CEOs who were attending a breakfast for a local chamber and to hear the state's governor speak. I told him to focus on people who were alone and do what he could to make them comfortable.

He attended with such a level of anxiety he could barely think. He spotted one individual standing alone and rushed over to introduce himself. He gave him his card and asked the individual's name. "I'm the governor," he responded, much to my client's embarrassment. As the governor's body guards joined the conversation, it broke the ice, my client and governor discussed my client's career interests, and he ended up with an appointment with someone on the governor's staff. In the exercise sections there are several ideas for networking that are effective even if they don't involve governors.

You may want to look at *Activity Ten: How to Make Cold Calls*

The Plan: How to Use What You Have Learned About Chaos, Systems, and the Four Scans

"What time is it? You mean right now?"
Attributed to Yogi Berra

Yogi Berra's firm grasp of the obvious can help us. The time to start using the ideas outlined here is now.

Scan One) Momentum building: Do you accept responsibility for your success? Do you believe your dreams are worth the effort and that if you take action you can succeed?

Scan Two) Knowing what matters: Do you know what matters to you in your life and in the work that you do? Do those things matter enough to influence your behavior?

Scan Three) Synthesizing information: How are you keeping up with the world in general and your profession in particular? What are you doing to learn and create new knowledge?

Scan Four) Building synergistic relationships: What are you doing to build community and to help others through networking?

You should answer these questions for both the short term (tactically) and the long term (strategically). Tactical planning refers to immediate decision-making. Strategic planning refers to career development over time.

Tactical Planning and Decision-Making

Our day's activities are a series of decisions; some made intentionally, some made automatically. No one would want to use the four scans on every decision, as there simply isn't time. The more you use the scans, however, the more "tuned" your scanner will be to what matters, and the more your intuition will help create the kind of career you want. (Remember the role intuition plays in decision-making. If it doesn't feel right, employ the four scans.)

We all have our own definition about what makes a big decision and what is routine. For some of us a job change is routine, for others huge. Regardless of the magnitude of the decision, the process is the same:

1. What do I need to do to get started and to take charge? Is the effect of that decision something I value and can achieve?

2. What is important to me? How does the answer tie back to what really matters?

3. What information am I going to gather or create? How do I do my homework?

4. Who needs to help me with what I am about to do? Who will be affected by what I am about to do?

If we apply that model to our larger decisions, eventually we will apply it automatically to all that we do. Imagine, for example, that you have been asked to chair a new team about to tackle a particularly touchy issue important to the company. Here is what you might sort through as you consider your role:

1. How high is my confidence in my ability to chair this group? Can I pull it off? Will I enjoy being the chair, and do I really want the outcome this chairmanship will bring me? Will I have time in the face of my other tasks?

2. How does the team's project tie back to what I value? Will the committee compromise what really matters to me or does it reflect what really matters to me?

3. What information resources will I need, and will I be able to access those resources? Is there a training or research budget for this committee?

4. Who needs to be involved? Who will I help by chairing this committee? Will it help me reach my career goals?

Career Development

Career development refers to the growth of your productive activities over a lifetime. I was working with a group of young people, and one of the students listed a disjointed group of career titles she considered. I pushed her a bit, but she said she couldn't tell me what she really wanted as I might be angry.

It turned out that motherhood was her primary goal and would be the center of her career. She believed she was supposed to be the butcher, the baker, and the candlestick maker, or else it could not be a real career. I certainly wasn't angry. While she may or may not pursue paid employment, anything besides her primary career goal, motherhood, would play second fiddle. That's as it should be for her. Here, however, we focus on paid employment.

Like the landlocked submariner I mentioned earlier, the career pattern confidence builders—knowing what matters, intentional learning and synthesis, and networking are formed when we are young. Our four scans act like rudders, steering us to the serendipity we create for ourselves.

They will reform, take shape, and re-form throughout our lives. Identifying those patterns takes some thought, but they are there. Returning to the four scans, I offer you a means for discovering your success patterns:

1. As you think back, when have you felt successful? When have you thought you were able to make a difference? What do those successes tell you about what you need to do to succeed in the future?

2. Think back on the times that you really enjoyed what you were doing. What skills were you using? What were the activities? What made the activity enjoyable? What elements of the enjoyable activity can you bring to the future?

3. How do you like to learn and handle information? How do you learn the best? What do you do to stay current in your field? How do you access information outside of your field? Do you look for information in odd places?

4. How do you network? Do you belong to professional groups that you take part in on a regular basis? Do you attend meetings related to your work? Do you look for ways to help those that work with you? How do you build and nurture collegial relationships?

Conclusion: The Seeds of Success Exist Within You

I hope you realize now that the seeds of success already exist within you. But also realize that the seeds of resistance to success are there as well.

Take charge and understand what matters to you. As you continue to learn and create new knowledge, help others as you network. What you give comes back to you.

My approach to career development is as much a philosophy as it is a set of techniques. You are not looking for a job. You are looking for opportunities to solve problems to help others.

Activities Section

The following sets of activities can be done in any sequence or you can select the activities that appear helpful to you. They all facilitate the scanner tuning process that leads to better organized serendipity. If you are working with a group, an acquaintance on the same career odyssey, or a career counselor, these activities can be especially effective.

Activity One: Reality Check

The *Reality Check* activity compares what you think matters to your actual behavior. This journaling exercise will help you reflect on the congruence between what you want to believe you value and what your behaviors say that you value. Do this exercise over time as it requires reflection. It asks for the degree of control you believe you have over the time you spend on any activity.

- If you are incarcerated, for example, you may not be able to pursue a passion for mountain climbing.
- If you value time with your family but never see them, what is going on? What needs to change?

Describe what you want your life to be. How do you want to spend your time? You may want to look at varying the realms of your live I list below. Some activities cannot occur daily and some activities may be things you would like to do later. You are not establishing an alibi to account for each waking moment, but rather a chance to reflect on your actual values, goals, and your efforts to achieve the life you prefer.

Activity Preference – How you want to spend your time	Amount of time each day (column adds up to 100%)
Physical (sedentary, physically active, high risk activities, etc.)	

Level of control: high - manageable - low	
Social (out every night, hermit, sort of people you would prefer for your associates, etc.) Level of control: high - manageable - low	
Spiritual (life of prayerful contemplation, serenity, agnostic, involvement in organized religion, paganism) Level of control: high - manageable - low	
Relationships (deeply committed to one person, free of entanglements, surrounded by family) Level of control: high - manageable - low	
Vocational (ideal paid employment, volunteer, predictable, varied, professional, artistic	

commitment) Level of control: high - manageable - low	
Avocational (hobbies you would pursue) Level of control: high - manageable - low	
Civic involvement (work in the community, engaged in the political process) Level of control: high - manageable - low	

Actual Activities – How did you spend your time?	Amount of time each day (column adds up to 100%)
Physical (sedentary, physically active, high risk activities, etc.)	

Social (out every night, hermit, sort of people you would prefer for your associates, etc.)	
Spiritual (life of prayerful contemplation, serenity, agnostic, involvement in organized religion, paganism)	
Relationships (deeply committed to one person, free of entanglements, surrounded by family)	

Vocational (ideal paid employment, volunteer, predictable, varied, professional, artistic commitment)	
Avocational (hobbies you pursue)	
Civic involvement (work in the community, engaged in the political process)	

Activity Two: Internal and External Scans

The list of questions below helps you focus your two internal and two external scans. Once you have completed the scan, you will have a list of "To Do" items. If one area needs more work than the other three, pay attention. If you are working with a coach or counselor, bring the list to your next session.

Self-Talk for Scan One: Scan my willingness to take responsibility for my career

	Do not need to work on this area	Need help in this area	Priority, need help now
How would I rate my level of self-confidence?	Strong	OK	I am not confident
What will it take to increase my self-confidence?			
Am I willing to accept responsibility for the outcome of my job search?	Yes	Some	None
How do I demonstrate my willingness to take responsibility for my future?			
How much control do I have over my future?	I control my future	Not sure	Rely entirely on others
How can I take more control over my future?			

If I try, what is the likelihood of achieving career success?	I will succeed	I can succeed if I try	Too many obstacles
What can I do to help myself succeed?			
Do I value the goals I have set for myself?	I highly value the goals I have set	I would like to succeed	I am not sure about my goals
What will success look like for me?			
Do I initiate self-help activities or wait for others to help me?	I jump in	I hesitate	I wait for direction from others
How do I know that I am taking initiative for managing my future?			
What is my capacity for personal leadership?	I am self-disciplined	I usually can be self-directed	Prefer outside support
Can I motivate myself?			
What is my capacity for ambiguity?	I can tolerate uncertainty	I can deal with some	I hate uncertainty
How do I react when I am not sure what the future holds?			

| Overall, how do I rate myself in my first scan? | Fine | Need help | Need a lot of help |

What do I want to change about my attitudes toward taking control of my future?

Self-Talk for Scan Two: Scan my understanding of what matters to me in the work that I do and the sort of life I hope to lead

	Do not need to work on this area	Need help in this area	Priority, need help now
Do my work behaviors reflect my values?	Always	Maybe	I am not sure
Are there values I need to revisit or behaviors that I need to change?			
Can I describe my values?	Always	Maybe	Not sure
My values (list):			
Can I describe my preferred skills?	Always	Maybe	Not sure
My preferred skills (list):			
Can I describe my favorite abilities?	Always	Maybe	Not sure
The abilities I most like to use (list):			
Can I describe my preferred work environments?	Always	Maybe	Not sure
My preferred work environments (list):			

Do my values represent <u>my</u> views, or are they adopted from some other source?	Yes	Maybe	Not sure
My values came from (list the sources):			
When I look back over my paid and unpaid work experiences, can I identify what makes me successful?	Yes	Maybe	Not sure
I tend to be successful when:			
How I rate myself overall in this category	Fine	Need help	Need a lot of help
What do I want to learn about my skills, values, interests, and abilities?			

Self-Talk for Scan Three: Scan my approach to understanding my environment and gathering knowledge as a life-long learner

	Do not need to work on this area	Need help in this area	Priority, need help now
How do I react to new information?	Love to learn new things	Learn what I need to learn	Prefer to avoid new information
Where and how do I access new information?			
What is my preferred learning style?	Certain I know	Maybe I know	I don't know my learning style
Where and how have I learned the best?			
What is my capacity for open-ended information or directions?	I thrive when there is lack of clarity	I usually can deal with some uncertainty	I am uncomfortable with uncertainty
How do I react when I am expected to interpret directions?			

What is my capacity for remaining open to information that contradicts what I think is true about me?	I am challenged	Depends on the contradiction	I become defensive
How open am I to changing my mind about my beliefs?			
At what level do I personalize information?	I usually see how information relates to me	I understand once I think about new information	*I understand once someone explains how it relates to me*
Do I make an effort to incorporate new information into my daily activities?			
Do I know how to continue my formal education (i.e. earn a degree)	Already working on a degree	I think I know how to start	*I don't know how to register for a degree program*
What are my feelings about continuing my formal education?			

I know how to find workshops and courses that relate to my area of interest	Yes	Maybe	No
How do I rate myself as a lifelong learner?			
I know where to find career and job information about careers that interest me.	Yes	Maybe	No
Do I know how to use government, Internet, and informal resources?			
I know where to look for my next job.	Yes	Maybe	No
Do I know how the hidden job market works?			
How effective am I at basic research?	Love doing research	I can look things up	What is research?
Am I a good problem solver? Can I find information when I have questions?			

I know how to research companies	Yes	Maybe	No
Do I know several ways to look into the inner workings of any company?			
How do I rate myself overall in this category	Fine	Need help	Need a lot of help
What do I want to change about the way I learn?			

Self-Talk for Scan Four: Scan for willingness to create opportunities for myself through networking and to continually build mutually beneficial relationships

	Do not need to work on this area	Need help in this area	Priority, need help now
How easy is it for me to form interdependent relationships?	I get along with almost everybody	I can get along with most people	I prefer to depend on myself
How comfortable am I having to depend on others and having them depend on me?			
Do I have an entrepreneurial attitude toward my career plans?	I view my employers and my colleagues as customers	I take personal responsibility for exceeding the expectations of others	I do my job as is expected of me
Do I manage my career as though it is a small business?			

How am I at networking?	I enjoy meeting and talking with new people	I am comfortable meeting new people if I have to	I prefer not to go to gatherings where I don't know anybody
What happens to me when I request something from someone I don't know well?			
Can I identify different ways to network and for different reasons?	I have a wide range of networking activities	I think I network as well as most	*I have no idea how to start*
How good am I at getting out and meeting people?			
I know how to write a focused resume	Confident	Would like some help	I do not know where to begin
Is my resume like an obituary or like a marketing piece?			
I know how to write an effective cover letter	Confident	Would like some help	I do not know where to begin
Can I get people's immediate attention with my cover letter?			

I am confident in my interviewing skills	Confident	Would like some help	I do not know where to begin
Can I put forth a good impression in interviews?			
I am confident in my appearance and manners	Confident	Would like some help	I do not know where to begin
How are my personal appearance and mannerisms helping me?			
I am confident in my ability to negotiate for a salary	Confident	Would like some help	I do not know where to begin
What am I worth and am I willing to ask for it?			
I know how to reach "insiders" for any company that I want to work for.	Confident	Would like some help	I do not know where to begin
Can I use a series of contacts to access insider information?			
How I rate myself overall in this category	Fine	Need help	Need a lot of help
What do I want to change about the way I market and network?			

Activity Three: Feelings Scale

What do you do when you're stuck? First, check your emotional inertia. What are you feeling as you look at approaching some task?

Frozen in fear	Reluctance and resistance	Delay as long as possible	Acceptance, just do it	Can hardly wait to get started
1-2	3-4	5-6	7-8	9-10

Typical job search tasks we might avoid::

- Calling my references
- Calling people I know
- Telling my spouse I am making a career change
- Identifying my transferable skills
- Organizing my finances

- Asking for a raise
- Going to see a career coach
- Finding out what the first step is that I need to take.
- Deciding what I want to do
- Reviewing my evaluations

- Taking a course
- Putting my resume in order
- Realizing the need to change something in my job
- Making out a job application
- Clinging to security needs

What would it take to get you to move? What would move you to action?

Alice hated making cold calls. She would take a beating before making a cold call. I asked her on a scale of one to 10, 10 being totally confident, where she would be. She described herself as a two.

I then asked her what it would take to get her up to a four. She thought for a moment, and said, "If I had someone's name I could use, as in, 'Fred suggested I call and talk to you,' the call would be easier." I asked what it would take to get her from a four to a seven.

She thought a bit longer, and concluded that if she was confident she could solve the problems the business needed to solve, she would be a "seven." Cold calls were not suddenly a joy to do, but at least she had a strategy to make them a bit more approachable.

Alice hated the thought of making cold calls and could not make herself get started.	Alice would be more comfortable with cold calls if she knew a name she could use as an introduction.		Alice could move ahead with her calls if she knew how she could help a perspective employer.	She may never be a "10," but at least she can accomplish the task.
1-2	3-4	5-6	7-8	9-10

What are you willing to do?

Take a look at what you need to do next to take charge of your career. The table of issues might bring to mind some of the challenges you face. Be certain to break any major tasks into smaller steps such as I outline in the table below.

Manageable Steps
Challenge: Ask for a raise

- Find out what the scale is for your industry and your company.
- Organize your accomplishments according to how much you helped the company make or save.
- Organize your performance evaluations.
- Prepare a description of what you will do for the company in the immediate future.
- Be certain you understand what keeps the decision makers up at night and how you can help them resolve their concerns.

Challenge: Find a new career

- Take time to describe your ideal job.
- Look into taking an interest assessment.
- Find an organization that provides career coaching.
- Interview people who hold jobs that look interesting to you.
- See if your company has career-development services.

What emotions do you experience when you consider taking action? What would it take to get you to move to action? Go back to Alice's chart and complete one of your own. Outline a plan that will help you move up the spectrum from "Frozen with fear" to "Can hardly wait." Most of the resources you need will be in one of these categories:

- People who can act as a sounding board or give you support
- People who are experts
- People who can provide you information or help with "intelligence gathering"
- Information about the challenge you are tackling

- Physical resources such as money or transportation

You may want to use this format to organize your strategy:

- First Big Problem
    - First manageable step
        - People resources
        - Information resources
        - Material resources
    - Plan of action – what I will do about this first step

You know you have a good plan when you have one good action you are willing to take. Finding that action may take some thought, but it will make the difference between stagnation and success. Keep looking for manageable steps until you find something you are willing to do. Make that first step and then go to the next manageable step. Just remember: Little actions can bring big changes. But first you have to start.

Activity Four: Your "Go-for-It Gauge"

What would it take to voluntarily jump into an ice cold pool of water on a chilly fall morning? What result would make it desirable? How likely would your plunge into the pool bring you the results you want?

Maybe a quick dip into ice water is part of your daily ritual or, at the other extreme, you cannot imagine any reward that could draw you into that water. The cold water is a way to explore the energy you are willing to invest in career growth, and how much responsibility you will accept for your career success.

What will it take to get you into our metaphorical pool of water (or jump into a new career opportunity)? How much momentum would you generate if there is a pretty rock at the bottom of the pool (representing limited desire on your part), and you probably couldn't reach the rock if you tried (representing limited confidence on your part)? Not much, I imagine.

You would give up before you tried. On the other hand, imagine a pot of gold at the bottom (representing something you want to own), and you know that with one quick dip you could bring the treasure to land (representing a high level of confidence on your part).

Theoretically, you would soon be dripping wet, teeth chattering from the cold while you admired your prize. We can enter all sorts of variables such as a pot of gold in a pool of piranhas or a shiny rock you need only bend over to pick up—with their impacts on how much energy you would expend.

The energy we are willing to put into a particular project depends upon the *desirability* of the goal and our *level of confidence* in our success. The more we want the outcome and the more we believe we can succeed, the more effort we will put into working toward the goal.

Now we'll put the idea behind the pool story with the "Go-for-It Gauge." Think of some small task you anticipate beginning or something you have done recently. Pick a project that is recent and uncomplicated. The more desirable the goal and the more optimistic you are about it, the more confidence and commitment you will put into it.

I offer an example to help you get started:

Go-for-It Gauge

Goal or outcome of the project:
Install a dead-bolt lock on the back door.

Desirability of the goal. What makes this project worth the effort?

1. This lock will make our home more secure, and I love these little projects.
2. I can save money if I do the job myself.
3. I can demonstrate my prowess as a handyman.

What might compromise the value of the goal? How might I decide the outcome is not worth the effort?

1. I'm not certain that this lock is really necessary.
2. It will mean we have to mess about with an extra key.
3. It may mar the appearance of the door.

Sources of confidence: What experiences have I had or what information do I possess that leads me to believe I can complete this project?

1. I have done this sort of thing before.
2. I am usually pretty successful with fixing and making things.
3. My wife has encouraged me to install the lock.
4. I will have a reason to buy a new tool, and I love new tools.

Perceived barriers and resistance: What issues lead me to doubt my ability to complete this project? I am afraid I will ruin the door if I try to drill a hole in it.
1. I do not have time, and if I hurry I will make a mess of the job.
2. If I make a mess, we will need a new door.
3. I'm not sure that we really need to spend all of this money.
4. I am too tired to bother.

What I might do to sabotage my efforts? How have I compromised my success in the past?

1. Procrastinate.
2. In order to have it over with, I might rush and do a sloppy job and just settle for less than my best work.
3. Make excuses why I can't do the job.

I have reviewed my level of momentum and the desirability of the goal, and here is what I will do:

1. Carefully read the directions when I come home Monday evening.
2. On Tuesday evening, I will apply the template that came with the directions and be certain I have all the tools I need.
3. Since I have more time on Wednesday, I can actually drill the required holes and install the lock.

As we look back over my "Go-for-It Gauge," I have evaluated the outcome and considered my experiences with such projects. It's as though I were two people, stepping back and imagining how I will approach this project and what I can do to be committed. If I am, I know what I need to do.

By developing this chart, I confronted my reluctance to drag out all my tools and get started, and I also realized that it wasn't that big a deal.

Notice that in the "What I will do?" section, I broke things down into manageable steps. . On the other hand, I could have realized the project was more than I wanted to tackle and called a carpenter. I developed the momentum I needed, and we have a new lock.

As you select a project to tackle with our "Go-for-It Gauge," please keep in mind we are addressing career concerns. on.

Your turn: Complete the chart for a project you have done or are considering.

Go-for-It Gauge

Goal or outcome of the project:
_____
_____
_____
_____

Desirability of the goal. What makes this project worth the effort?
_____
_____
_____
_____

What might compromise the value of the goal? How might I decide the outcome is not worth the effort?
_____
_____
_____
_____

Sources of confidence. What experiences have I had or what information do I possess that leads me to believe I can complete this project?
_____
_____
_____
_____

**Perceived barriers and resistance. What issues lead me to doubt that I can complete this project? What

external influences or personal issues may cause me to fail?

_____
_____
_____
_____

What might I do that would sabotage my efforts? How have I done things to compromise my success in the past?

_____
_____
_____
_____

I have reviewed my level of momentum and the desirability of the goal, and here is what I will do:

_____
_____
_____
_____

Activity Five: Tips for Momentum Building

Pause to separate your heart from your head: I am not recommending one over the other since that would be pointless. To be totally analytical or totally emotional is not the goal here. The goal is awareness.

When under stress, our natural instinct is to run if we can or attack if we are cornered. When that "flee or fight" emotion emerges, step back and observe what you are doing, thinking, and feeling.

Understand the source of your emotions. At times, we can use our heads to coach ourselves through emotions that might otherwise immobilize us. Under stress, we may find ourselves reacting destructively or note that we are out of control and need to stop all action and do nothing. I recall one fellow who was so distraught over his job loss that he forgot how to drive.

He had a right to be upset, and it was not a good time for him to drive. Fear and nervousness are gifts that generate adrenaline and tell us it is time to focus and take immediate care of ourselves.

Develop an action plan: Developing and pursuing a manageable action plan can help build momentum and overcome the inertia of lost confidence. Mental health clinicians working with severely depressed people, for example, will break task contracts into small steps.

You can apply the same strategy to yourself when you have trouble getting started. Begin with what you are truly willing to do. Identify the tentative goal and then start with what you are truly willing to do. Break the goal into manageable steps.

Goals might include making a phone call, composing a letter, looking for a piece of information, or making an appointment. Identify one step you will do today and do it. If you find yourself not following through, consider that all behavior is goal-oriented, including avoidance behavior.

If you are not moving, what are you trying to avoid? Successful change calls for looking perceived barriers in the eye. Recalibrate the barrier into pieces you are willing to address and get moving. You may want to ask for feedback from a support group as you develop your steps.

Learn to use positive self-talk: Listen to how you talk to yourself. Are you encouraging? Do you coach yourself through small steps? We can be both our own best friends and our worst enemies.

Think back on someone you found encouraging. How did he or she talk to you? If no one immediately comes to mind, imagine how you wish someone had encouraged you, and let your inner voice use their phrases, maybe even the sound of their voice, to cheer you on.

Do not ever put yourself down. When you do, you diffuse responsibility for your destiny. Sometimes you hurt because of what you have done, but do not stick more pins in the wound. Above all, avoid saying, "I told you so," even if it is true.

Bring a positive attitude to the "Monday Morning Whine:"
Monday morning is a major excuse to whine. If you really want to build momentum, wipe out deliberate indulgence in the "what can you expect—it's Monday" lament.

As self-organizing systems, we are always exchanging information to adjust our career self-concept. To build momentum, we need to build a positive career self-concept by keeping that exchange positive.

One word of caution: Complaining is our native tongue. So your enthusiasm and positive attitude may not be well-received at first. Stick with your determination to be positive, and eventually it will catch on with others. Leave complaining about Mondays to Garfield.

Get involved: One member of a career group we conducted described her time between jobs as "busy being busy." She got up every morning, dressed for work, and went out and volunteered. She kept moving. Not only did her volunteer activities help keep up her momentum, she began getting paid for her contributions, and she expanded her networks. She vowed that every day she would do one thing to get out of the house and make a contribution somewhere in her community.

Use selective optimism: Is your cup half full or is it half empty? During an outplacement workshop one of the participants observed, "I've needed this kick in the pants for a long time. I'm going back to school and learn to do what I truly want to do." We can apply an adaptation of his observation to transitions in your life. Identify the change that you see happening in your life right now.

The Personal Benefits and Opportunities of Change: Make two lists. On the first, jot down the personal benefits you will derive from the change you are confronting. On the second list, write the opportunities the situation creates.

Remember to think about what you are moving to, not what you are leaving behind. If negatives are the first things that come to mind, go back and turn them into positives. This is not to say you should bury the upsets, but the exercise focuses on positive energy.

We use this exercise with our outplacement groups, and I offer some examples from the lists that one group generated when they were told their jobs would be terminated in three months:

Personal Benefits of Change	Opportunities Provided
• I have put off going back to school; now I will go.	• I am going to turn my hobby into a business.
• This job took a lot of time from my family; it's time to look for something less time-consuming.	• Other companies will fill the niche left by the downsizing, and they will need people like me.
• There are skills I would like to use that I have set aside; this is my chance to put them back in my resume and market them elsewhere.	• I know they still need to get the work done; I could offer consulting services while exploring other options.

Share positive energy with others: Getting self-absorbed when we suffer the pain that accompanies confusion or indecision burns up energy we should direct toward the future. Rather than move ahead, our overloaded emotions cause us to stall, and we lose momentum.

A young woman told me her career had stalled until her daughter was born. Before her daughter's birth, she was obsessed with finding direction and totally focused on herself. When she concentrated on her daughter, the mother's career direction became clear. While she was totally focused on her own pain, she could not move.

Extending support to others requires a deliberate effort: Do not assume you are already supportive. If we ask most people whether they show appreciation to others, most will claim that they do.

I was conducting a program using the Myers-Briggs Type Indicator with couples when one husband said he always showed appreciation for what his wife did. His wife looked at him in astonishment and retorted that he never showed appreciation.

At that point, the chase was on with no end in sight in the "who appreciates whom and how" contest. Each member of every couple in the group saw the same truth but interpreted it was differently. You are challenged to find a balance between constant, shallow emotional gush and chronic neglect by looking at specific behaviors to reinforce in a marriage.

Start with good manners: If demonstrating good manners is as far as you get, you will have done well. If you compliment others , be specific. Avoid statements "good boy" or "nice job."

Avoid comparisons and picking favorites. Instead, cite specific examples such as, "That font you used made the report easy to read" or "I like your hair that way." Above all else, be sincere. Compliment people because you like something, not simply to manipulate.

Do not use acts of kindness as a test to see if you get

something back: You will, but it will not be immediate. Your positive acts will raise the quality of life around you, as you begin organizing your life around getting positive results.

Marilyn Moats Kennedy, author of many career-related materials, once observed that no one wants to hire a wet mess. Blaming others for your troubles can create the appearance that you are a "wet mess." Certainly the blame for any negative circumstances troubling you can be placed elsewhere, and your attitude may be understandable, but it will not help to complain. It can only make you less attractive as a perspective employee.

Sources of help for building momentum: There are many sources of uplifting material readily available. Be selective as not all of it works for all people. What I find inspirational may leave you annoyed.

For example, I find looking at the shape of trees relaxing and inspirational. Some may look at trees and end up bird watching, another source of inspiration.

One fellow I know would look at trees and convert them to the value of lumber and pulp wood. Whether you convert your visions to patterns or cordwood does not matter; just know what works for you and do it.

Below I list some ideas that may help with momentum building:

- Books that address your areas of career interest as well as self-help literature: Reading such books helps you identify your level of commitment. This book falls into that category. Ask people you know what they found useful. *Leadership and the New Science* by Margaret Weatley relates quite well to the lessons found in this book. *Journey to Center* by Thomas Crum suggests ways to personalize the self-organizing theme in this book, although he does not address the topic directly. I find inspiration in learning new things, so my readings range from *Dave Pelz's Short Game Bible* to *Dynamic Patterns: The Self-Organization of Brain and Behavior* by J.A. Kelso.

- Newspapers and websites that offer career information: Content ranges from actual job offers to guides for career change. Several newspapers have career assistance online. Some examples:
  Washington Post
  http://www.washingtonpost.com/career-advice/

  Wall Street Journal
  http://www.wsj.com/public/page/news-career-jobs.html

  USA Today "Career Center"
  www.usatoday.com/careers/ask/ourcouns.htm

  Career Magazine
  www.careermag.com/

  BestJobsUSA.com
  www.bestjobsusa.com/

  Monster
  http://www.monster.com/

- Websites that offer inspiration: Some sites have inspirational quotes or stories. Many are of a spiritual nature. I enjoy www.mrmd.com/comf. This website reminds us to put temporary setbacks in perspective and get moving again.

- Websites with humor: Laughter is indeed the best medicine. There is some evidence that laughter releases endorphins from your brain. Endorphins are a natural pain killer and chemically related to morphine. They make you feel good, so know what makes you laugh and seek it out.

Some corporations hire humor consultants to blend healthy humor into the workday. Check out the home page for the American Association for Therapeutic Humor as a start to finding websites (www.aath.org/). Other sites to visit:
www.humormatters.com/

www.humor.com/

www.netfunny.com/rhf/

- Self-help web sites: As aggravating as a job search can be, work on building and keeping a positive attitude. Some sites I like follow:

Via Character discusses character preferences, including a survey to help identify your strengths. The free personality strengths assessment can help build the vocabulary you need for the important work of scanner tuning.
http://www.viacharacter.org/survey/Account/Register

Happify has games and activities designed to chase the blues. While a bit simplistic, I believe the activities can really help. They certainly help you scan your attitude and take responsibility for cheering yourself up--not always an easy task during a career change.
http://www.happify.com/

Positive Psychology News gathers information on the growing *positive psychology* movement. The ideas on this site work.
http://positivepsychologynews.com

Insight Timer offers a timer and guided meditations for some constructive and habilitating respite care from the tyranny of our own thoughts. Meditation has proven to have multiple health and behavioral benefits. This website is a good way to get started and stick with it. I

find the guided meditations by Tara Brach helpful for beginners. I learned about the site from reading *10% Happier: How I Tamed the Voice in My Head, Reduced Stress Without Losing My Edge, and Found Self-Help That Actually Works--A True Story* by Dan Harris.
https://insighttimer.com/

- Civic, religious, and social groups: Those that reflect your interests help build momentum as they keep you in touch with the local work environment. The camaraderie can supporting you through discouraging times. Develop a sense of mission through volunteer work and, of course, build those networks. Spirituality can enhance the sense that we are all part of something larger than ourselves, which serves as one major source of momentum.
- Colleagues, friends, and family: Remember to form affiliations with an eye to the type of energy they provide. Do not let negative people drag you down. If you cannot avoid them, cheer them up.

Activity Six: Tuning your Scanner with an Awareness of Your Temperament Preferences

Review the five scales listed below and underline the words that represent your temperament preferences. Temperament is how you view your character and disposition as you interact with others. Consider your preferences when you are under pressure. When we feel stressed, we tend to reveal our "default" behaviors. This exercise can help you discover and scan these default preferences. Underlining the terms that describe you builds your vocabulary, which helps you scan temperament preferences.

In each scale highlight your preferred descriptors. You will probably select more descriptors from one side than the other, but that's fine. Have someone who knows you well complete the scale for you. You do not need to own the results they offer, but it may be useful to reflect on their view of your preferred behaviors. As you add these descriptors to your self-awareness, you will be better at managing your own behaviors as you interact with others. You can also use your favorite descriptors to answer that pesky interview question, "Describe yourself."

Please avoid be too judgmental. For example, compassion (right hand side of "Openness") may be seen as desirable. Most of us are capable of caring for others. If you are guided by compassion, highlight it. On the other hand, if logic dictates your interaction with others, you may not highlight it.

Agreeableness

I am quick to voice my opinion in a team environment and say what needs to be said. I assert myself in order to advance in the company. Others may see me as unfriendly and uncooperative, but I am focused on what's best for the company. Preferred descriptors: Opinionated, dogmatic, political, stubborn, obstinate, uncompromising, strict, set in my ways, assertive, self-assured, emphatic, insistent, positive, aggressive, forward, attentive, absorbed, intensive, engrossed, concentrated, single-minded, driven, resolute, persistent, pessimistic	I place a high value getting along with others. I generally have an optimistic view of human nature. Preferred descriptors: Flexible, timid, hopeful, positive, expectant, enthusiastic, buoyant, friendly, amicable, sociable, cordial, kind, genial, considerate, good natured, humorous

Conscientiousness

I prefer internal measures of achievement and spontaneity. Preferred descriptors: introspective, contemplative, self-	I tend to act dutifully and aim for achievement against measures of outside expectations. I prefer planned activities rather than exhibiting spontaneous behavior.

analytical, soul searching, impulsive, unstructured, extemporaneous, instinctive, unrehearsed, carefree, spontaneous, informal, ingenious, unplanned	Preferred descriptors: scrupulous, thorough, meticulous, careful, diligent, punctual, precise, fussy, enjoy attention to detail, obedient, loyal, submissive, devoted, respectful, intentional, calculated, organized, prepared, deliberate

Emotionally Reactive

I tend to be less emotionally reactive. I am calm, emotionally stable, and free from persistent negative feelings Preferred descriptors: calm, impassive, undramatic, unemotional, inexpressive, deadpan, cool, aloof, remote, reserved, indifferent, distant, detached, unapproachable, proud lofty, independent, autonomous	I can easily experience negative emotions such as anger, anxiety, or depression. I may be more vulnerable to stress than people around me. Preferred descriptors: Expressive, passionate, fervent, warm, enthusiastic, sensitive, emotionally needy, supportive, respectful, dependent

Openness

I prefer the straightforward over the complex and ambiguous. I prefer familiarity over novelty. I tend to be conservative. Preferred descriptors: straightforward, frank, forthright, candid upfront, direct, clear-cut, uncomplicated, traditional, conventional, conformist, careful, cautious	I appreciate unusual ideas, imagination, and variety of experience. I am aware of the feelings of others. I tend to be liberal. Preferred descriptors: unfamiliar, atypical, unordinary, unfamiliar, scarce, uncommon, change, variability, variation, diversity, empathetic, benevolent, compassionate

Extroversion

I tend to be quiet, low-key, deliberate, and less involved in the social world. I am not shy. I simply need less stimulation than other people and more time alone. I am more comfortable working by myself. Preferred descriptors: discreet, unobtrusive, peaceful, tranquil, thoughtful, cautious, wary, measured, methodical, purposeful, complex, insulated, solitary, quiet, soloist	I prefer to seek out stimulation and the company of others. I am usually enthusiastic and action-oriented. I enjoy being with people and participating in social gatherings. Preferred descriptors: Inspired by others, excited, eager, animated, communal, social, people person, talkative, team spirited

Activity Seven: Tuning Your Scanner with a Career Experience Timeline

Jobs are not made up of titles but rather the components of those jobs. As you move towards doing what you want, you need to examine components to build your next job. What matters to you in each of them?

Look back at past jobs and volunteer experiences and see what you would like to bring into the future. You might even review jobs you might like to have to further help you focus on your preferred future. This exercise helps you with that second scan—what matters to you in the work you do.

Once you know what matters, you will tune your scanner to find opportunities to pursue your passions. This step is critical to "organizing serendipity." You will be more likely to increase your luck if you practice focusing on what you want to do.

In the activity below, make a list of every job you have ever had under the job/volunteer column. You may not have space enough here, so use more paper. Include jobs you desire. The results may not be practical. At age eight, for example, I wanted to be a cowboy but I'm allergic to horses. I still would like to be a cowboy but I'm still allergic to horses. I was a saloon singer in the years immediately after college when I couldn't find a job to support my wife and me. I succeeded in earning a modest income, but my limited performing abilities offered us few enticing opportunities.

Turn to the online version of the *Occupational Handbook* (http://www.bls.gov/ooh/) for a generic and detailed description of your real and desired employment experiences.

Go get lots of paper, copy this form, and use it to make a list of past jobs. Describe the following for each job. Writing all this done will really help stimulate your thinking and start tuning that scanner:

Job/Volunteer Activities:
What did you do and how did you spend your time:
Describe in as much detail as possible what you did to earn your money. Many people do not realize how much they know. This is your opportunity to reflect on the activities you performed and then identify the activities you preferred most.
Accomplishments:
Describe, in measurable terms if possible, what you accomplished. You might use measures such as money, time, units, number of people, number of incidents, or other key metrics. Paint a picture that helps you identify your strengths.
Benefits to the company:
Every job helps make money, save money, or help the company look good. How did you help provide a revenue stream? What ideas saved money? What did you do to polish the corporate image? This section may repeat some of your accomplishments.
Skills you liked using:
You know how to do many things. List the things you know how to do. You may want to list the skills you would like to use again and those you would prefer not using again.

Work environment:
I know one worker who earned an excellent salary in a manufacturing facility but quit after a camping trip. He discovered he wanted to work outdoors. Picture all the environments you have worked in and describe them.
People you liked working with:
Relationships shape the view we have of our work. Some prefer to come to work and be polite, but simply not interact on a personal level. Some see their colleagues as a circle of friends. Some prefer to work with people like themselves. Others want diversity.
Style of supervision that worked best for you:
Think back on the bosses you have had and describe them. Why did you favor one supervisor over another?
Degree of responsibility:
How much responsibility rested on your shoulders? Did you have someone reporting to you? Could your responsibility be measured in monetary terms? Did you have the kind of responsibility that a teacher or health practitioner might have for someone else's well-being?
Satisfaction with the income you earned:
Most people want more than they have, but as you think back over your past jobs, how did you feel about the amount of money you earned?
What would you like to change?
Look at each job in turn and think about what you would have changed about that job to make it more desirable.

Why did you leave?
The answer to this question is pretty straightforward; however, ask the question so you can avoid any problems in the future.
What strengths did you bring to the job?
What made you a stellar employee and what strengths from the past would you want to offer a future employer?

Activity Eight: Tuning Your Scanner with Your Ideal Job Description

If you don't know what you are looking for, you probably won't find it. Clarifying what gets you out of bed in the morning and eager to go to work leads you to those serendipitous contacts that lead to career growth and satisfaction. As a result of your scanner tuning you will be able to explain to others what you are looking for with authority and confidence. In all probability, those opportunities have always been there; you just need to adjust your view of the world so that you can see them.

Remember, there are no coincidences.

Now that your career time line is complete, consider your future "ideal" job. Draw from your past, outlined above, to develop a feel for the future. You do not want a job simply doing what you can do; you want a job doing what you want to do. You may be making a radical change in your career and may not have any background to bring to this section. In that case, paint a picture of what you think you want. Consider your experience and look at the times when you thought you were at your best. This exercise is a bit like affirmative inquiry, which assumes you already have done the things that bring you the most satisfaction and success. Now combine those positive experiences in the ideal job description below.

Job Title:
You may not know the title as the job may not exist yet so you may not have a job title yet.
What did you do that you want to do again and how did you spend your time:
Draw from each job you listed above to paint a picture of how you would like to spend your time. If none of your past jobs offer any material, use hobbies, volunteer experiences, or draw from jobs you may have observed.
Accomplishments at the ideal job:
What do you want to accomplish? What difference do you want to make in your corner of the world?
Benefits to the company at the ideal job:
How will you help provide a revenue stream, reduce costs, or improve the corporate image?
Skills you would like to use at the ideal job:
Some may be skills you plan to learn or may have used outside of paid employment.
Work environment at the ideal job:
Picture all the environments you have worked in and describe the ideal one for you. Like other sections of this table, the environment you prefer may be entirely different from any in the past.
People you like working with:
You may like to work alone or prefer a crowd. What will these people be like?

Style of supervision you prefer:
How do you want to be supervised, or do you prefer to work as a team? You may prefer to work on your own.
Degree of responsibility:
Responsibility often means pressure. How much stress and responsibility will you tolerate or maybe even seek in the work that you do?
Salary Requirements:
Most people want more than they have, but as you think back over your past jobs, how did you feel about the amount of money you earned?

Activity Nine: Your Thirty-Second Commercial

What do you say when people ask what you are looking for as your next work assignment? Keep in mind that every work-related problem relates to making money, saving money, or helping the client company or you look good. A prospective employer or networking contact wants to understand how you will add value.

Example: Promising Futures is a career coaching and consulting firm focused on selective hiring, manager coaching, and personal career management as well as outplacement and retention services. In one instance, for example, we saved a company $250,000 by retaining a manager it might have lost. We offer a blended-delivery method: Internet, in-person, and over-the-phone. Our clients include some of the largest companies in this state, such as - - -, and our large repeat customer base underscores our success rate.

Delivering Your "Thirty-Second Commercial"

- What interests your listeners? Are your listeners there to hear how you will help an organization look good? If so, relax and deliver that message instead of focusing on yourself. Relate your key points to their interests if possible.
- Make sure your speech is right for your listeners. Have a "chum" message and a "laser" message. A "chum" message (like "chumming" for fish, or in this case, opportunities) is for your general audience, while your "laser" message is for potential employers or direct links to those employers. When you know what potential employers need, tailor your laser message for them.
- Keep it short and simple. The appropriate length varies according to setting. A networking session is not an interview, and you can avoid detail. In an interview, the details of your accomplishments will be important. Be aware of your audience's attention span. Sometimes "less is more."
- You may plan to keep your message to 30 seconds, but don't cram so much into the message that you have to rush. Take your time. Be conversational, as if talking with a group of friends.
- Make eye contact with your listeners.
- Practice your speech ahead of time. Pause in the right places to make eye contact and catch your breath. Let your commitment show.
- Remember the 70/30 rule. Let them do most of the talking about the skills you want to use and the problems you want to solve.

You cannot expect your audience to have more confidence in you than you can express in yourself.

Write Your Commercial

The the prompts below will help you to develop your 30-second commercial:

1. What do you do?

2. **What problems did you solve that the audience can relate to?**

3. **What is your ideal or typical work setting?**

4. **Offer an example of a past success or two.**

Activity Ten: How to Do Cold Calls

Cold calls are generally used to schedule an appointment with a decision maker to see if there is a match between what he or she needs and what you offer. Few people enjoy making cold calls. Here are some suggestions that can help you work through the process:

- First and foremost, remember you are not looking for a job, but rather an opportunity to solve problems. You <u>are not</u> asking for something (a position of weakness), but you <u>are</u> offering something (a position of strength). Consider that you can provide a needed service to your prospect, much like a good deal on water to someone in the desert.
- Second, have some idea what the company needs. Where is their pain? If you have done your homework, you know. Tailor your 30-second commercial to their pain.

- Third, try to find out who you will be talking to. Ideally, use someone on the inside to conduct some research for you. Often when you get one voice, he or she will pause and say, "Let me put you on hold," and then you get a new voice. The new voice says, "This is (mumble blather gasp). Can I help you?" You have just lost your prospect's name. Instead, ask for the name of whom you should talk to. That won't always work, and may even tip your hand that you are selling something, but at least you won't be left wondering, "Who was that masked man that just offered me an interview?"

- Fourth, If you can use the name of someone your prospect knows in your opening statement, all the better. "Alex suggested I talk to you..." or "I was talking to Frieda." Obviously, make certain Alex did make the suggestion or that you did talk to Frieda. Having a name in common with the prospect helps create a door into the conversation. I once read an article about a company in the *Wall Street Journal*, then left a message with the company that I had seen it, and thought we should talk. Astonishingly, they called back to find out what the article was about.

- Fifth, have your speech ready, but don't read it. Speak naturally. You do not want to sound like a poorly trained telemarketer. Remember, you are not selling something; you are offering them access to the resolution of some business problem. They need you!

- Sixth, learn to deal with rejection. They don't know you well enough to reject you personally, so consider it one more step toward "yes."

- Seventh, separate yourself from the call. Your worth as a human being does not ride on the call and nor does your future. There are alternatives, even if you have not discovered them yet. Experienced sales professionals know you do your best sales job if you convince yourself that your worth as a human being is not tied to the sale.

- Eighth, don't bother people you can't help.

Sample dialogue:

> "Could I speak with Johanna Anderson please?"
>
> "This is Johanna."
>
> "Johanna, this is Al Friedman. Sid Mansfield suggested I call you because I understand we have a common interest in

applying computer management to procurement. I have a procurement background and am very familiar with Microsoft Access and spreadsheets. I am currently seeking a position in that area and thought it would be to our mutual benefit if I could meet with you for 30 minutes to see if there is a match. If it sounds like I can help you, we'll go from there; otherwise I can be on my way. Do you have any appointment times available this week?"

The applicant here has a contact person, and Al knows how he can help solve a problem that Johanna needs solved. He also emphasizes his interest in common with Johanna, the prospect. It also moves Johanna to action so that Al is not wasting her time or his. You can adapt this model for your particular situation.

Worksheets and Ideas to Help You Manage Your Career and Your Life

The Keys to Your Future

Reminders to Help You Manage Your Career and Your Life

You are not looking for a job. You are looking for an opportunity to solve problems.
Emphasize what you bring to the job. Employers want people who can solve the problems they need solved. When you offer them something (your ability to solve the problems they need solved), you are in a position of strength.

You are always moving to something
It is easiest to focus on the stressors that you are trying to escape. Instead, focus on the goals you want to reach. Sell yourself as someone moving toward the solution to the problems.

The more you know the more you see
The better you understand what is important to you in the work that you do, the more opportunities you will see.

You are the entrepreneur of your own talents
Manage your career as though it were a small business; treat your employer like a good customer. Think of your career plan as a business plan and your job search as a marketing plan.

Drive up to the door and give them more than they expect, but leave the motor running
Be flexible. You must be ready to adapt and change.

Job security rests with knowing your skills, keeping them sharp, and knowing how to market them
The half-life of a new idea is about six months. You need to adapt your skills to embrace those new ideas as they emerge. The only thing that persists is your ability to solve problems.

Helping others helps you
Moving your attention away from your difficulties helps you avoid becoming self-absorbed. Employers want people who contribute; practice kindness every day in small ways. Start with acts of kindness for your family and on the highway. Be extra polite when under stress and let your good manners help you get back on your feet.

Again (with gusto) every job exists in order to help the company make money, save money, or look good
Learn all you can about the problems your perspective customer or employer needs to have solved. Then find evidence in your experiences that proves you can do these things.

A resume is your marketing tool

Your resume is not a file dump for everything you've ever done. It documents what you can do to solve the problems an employer has to solve.

Sell what you want to become, not what you've done

When you move on toward new opportunities (or try to create them), focus on the opportunities you want to. It is easy to default to the same old patterns based on your old skills.

Build a life while you are building a livelihood

What do you really want your life to look like? Life is more than your paid employment.

The successful career search never ends

Keep your entrepreneurial spirit alive, even when a job change is not needed.

Opportunities Are Everywhere
Downsizing May Be Your Opportunity

If your career is in transition, emphasize that you are moving to something rather than dwelling on your current trials and frustrations. I asked recently unemployed participants in outplacement workshops at several companies to list the opportunities transition offers, the challenges it presents, and the next action they need to take.

The following list represents their input:

Opportunities:	Challenges:
• Reduce the stress I had with my previous job • Learn new skills • Learn to apply my old skills in new ways • More time for family, hobbies, travel, self, and home projects • More time to just relax • Discover new career opportunities and choices • Time for reflection • More time with people I care about • Travel • Start a new career • Focus on new potential and challenge myself in new ways • Opportunity to relocate	• Learn more about my finances • Learn to manage my own time • Going back to work • Sharing space at home • Lose the excuse regarding time to live healthy • Marketing yourself • Lack of benefits • Social contacts • Uncertainty • Role change • Maintain lifestyle financially • Curtailing some plans and activities • Change my way of thinking • Opportunity to do more with less • Keep out of spouse's way • Losing contacts with co-

- to a wonderful new place
- Touch your heart's endeavors
- Do something different after 35 years
- Develop a better understanding of my spouse
- Do some volunteer work while trying out new skills
- Rediscover the things I enjoyed earlier in life
- Re-focus on what matters to me in my career
- Find a whole new career or just re-tinker what I have been doing
- Time to clean my closets
- Make more money
- Find more to enjoy

workers
- Self-motivation
- Find passion: I have too many interests
- Get organized
- Live on fixed income
- Self-discipline: getting out of bed in the morning
- Do more with less
- Continue feeling productive
- Self-motivation
- Role changes
- Overcoming fear of the unknown—learning to confront what I am afraid of
- Make my skills fit new requirements—what do perspective employers want and what will they value in my background?
- Decide where can I live, where do I want to live, balance money and quality of life
- Find fulfilling career that is personally meaningful and challenging—is what I do useful, beneficial, or useful to others?
- Meet ideals
- Just enough time to procrastinate
- What to tell my spouse
- Keep customer base

Actions:

Challenges:	What Do You Need to Do? What actions do you intend to take now? You may want to draw from what others have said.
• Get additional training and education • Put my finances in order and seek out someone to help with financial planning • Make a will • Develop a resume • Begin networking now • Learn how to spend less • Develop a support system for new ideas • Physical training • Gather information on how I can apply my skills to new applications • Decide: retire, continue in my field, or find new career • Check on the attitude I project • Network and reconnect, call friends • Attend job fairs and	**Financial & Career Plans**

professional meetings • Get my name out • Make a plan	
• Make a smooth transition for my family • Be especially supportive of my partner	**Personal Relationships**
• Recognize new opportunities and take advantage of them • Slow down to make good decisions • Accept the change in my life and look for the positive • Reorganize my life • Recognize self-worth • Soul searching • Put in perspective—how real or dire is the threat	**Attitudinal Adjustment and Motivation**
• Keep a journal • Talk with friends—they can offer empathy • Be able to relate to others • Focus on my mission • Relax and enjoy • Take a vacation • Keep busy	**Stress Management and Fun** We also asked participants to list strategies for coping with the stress of a job change:

How People Really Get Jobs

The more things change, the more they stay the same. The number one way that people still get jobs is through networking, including "social networking" as well as face-to-face contacts. All other methods remain a distant second. That does not mean you should ignore other strategies, but understand that you need to pursue a multi-pronged approach.

Here are some options:

Search Firms: Search firms collect a fee from your new employer. It is in their best interest to provide your new employer with the best hires possible. You will need more than one recruiter to place you. Be very clear on the work that you want to do and not everything that you can do. If recruiters know of a position that matches your skills, they will naturally want to place you and collect their fee.

Mailing: It is tempting to mass-produce one version of your resume and then flood the mails and cyberspace with the good news: You are available! Unfortunately, few will notice, and your resume goes nowhere. Companies receive unsolicited resumes on a regular basis, and they are generally ignored. If you want to try a mailing, focus on an individual who will be receptive to what you have to offer. Assert your unique qualities in light of the problems your audience needs to solve.

Job Fairs: Employers seeking workers for hard-to-fill positions often use job fairs. They collect resumes from prospects and follow up with an interview. Use job fairs to make contacts and follow up with a resume that reflects what you learned about the companies you talked with.

Temp and Employment Agencies: Temp and employment agencies are one option while you keep up the cash flow. They also can lead to permanent employment while you and the employer explore your relationship.

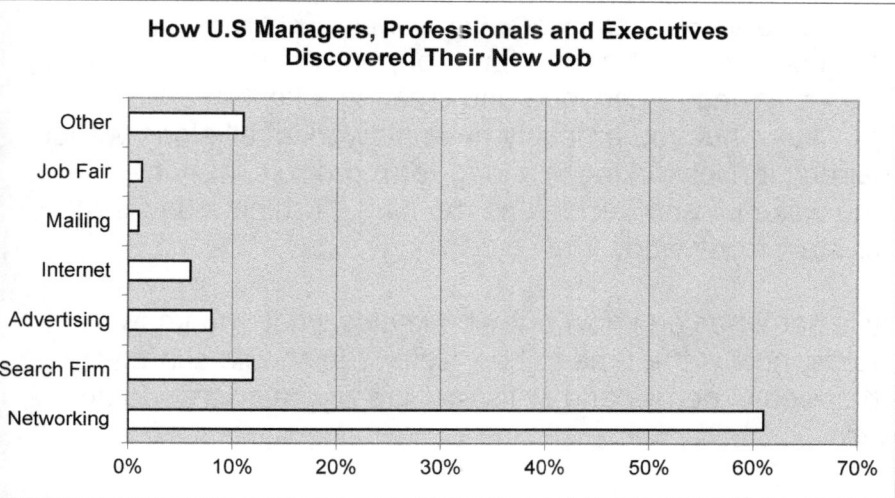

As shown in the chart, networking far outpaces other job-search techniques in helping people secure new jobs—nearly six times more effectively than any other strategy.

Effective Networking Techniques

Crisanne Kadamus Blackie
Director of the Career Center, University of Maine

Networking has image of asking for a job, bothering people, feeling fearful about having to network, and creating a knot in our stomach. Okay, but you probably have networked all along without even realizing it. Networking is a long-term process, not one in which you wake up and decide one morning, "I think today is the day I will start to network."

The key is not who you know but who knows what you know. In other words, now is the time to be visible. You should share with others that you expertise and skills that are of great value to an employer.

How Do I Get Started?

Pull out your address book and make a list of the people you know who may be of assistance. Hopefully you have this information captured electronically. They may be former colleagues, neighbors, family members, professional associates, church members, volunteer associates, members of parent groups, and classmates.

How Do I Decide Whom to Contact?

1. Start with those with whom you feel the most comfortable. It is wise to start with those who will lend support and help build your confidence.

2. Create a target list from your master list, including people who do what you would like to do, work at companies for whom you would like to work, or live in a location that you favor.

3. Prioritize your target list based upon your needs.

Where Do I Network?

Networking takes place in one of seven ways:

- Over the phone
- Through written correspondence—letter or email
- During one-on-one meetings
- At social events
- At planned networking events
- Gatherings of professional groups
- Chamber of Commerce meetings

Over the Phone: Some will be cold calls. That may make you nervous before you even start. Judy Rosemarin offers these tips in her article, *Networking Strategies for Shy Professionals*:

- Make calls when your energy is highest.
- Know what you want to say when calling. Develop a script that includes your key points and use it to make sure you mention important items.
- You may want to use a phone call to set up an appointment, thus moving to a one-on-one networking strategy.
- "When you make the appointment, mention that it won't take more than 10 minutes." (William Morin, *The Secret to Mastering Non-abusive Networking*)

Through Written Correspondence: If the phone terrifies you, consider the written word. Many individuals send a letter or an email prior to calling. Email tends to be quick and efficient, and people tend to respond.

When using email, remember to follow these guidelines:

- Follow the rules of email etiquette (e.g. all caps suggest yelling)
- Use proper grammar
- Always check your spelling
- Include contact information in your signature

- Remember that email is not confidential

One-on-One Meetings: Make sure you've given yourself reasonable time for self-appraisal and planning before taking up other people's time. If you find the interview going beyond the set time, acknowledge that you're running over and give your contact the option to continue. Keep your interview to the point.

We often associate networking with meeting someone in person at an office or an informal session over lunch. Although fairly common, that may produce some anxiety. So stay focused and to the point. By having a plan, you will know what to expect and remain in control.

Learn the names of secretaries. They may get your phone calls, and it helps to make them your allies.

Social Events: Social events include any business, professional, neighborhood, and community gathering. Have a strategy—what you want to achieve and how to achieve it. Don't expect to get a job offer, but gather business cards from those who can help. You canthen follow up with a meeting, phone call, or written correspondence.

- Wear your name tag on your right shoulder; it is easier for people to see as they shake your hand.
- You are not there to eat. You are there to mingle, meet, and network. It may help to have something in your hand, but do not get caught trying to balance a full-course meal while trying to exchange business cards and shake hands.
- It is very tempting to cling to your friends and colleagues; however, you are there to meet new people. Move away from the familiar.
- Give out business cards in order to get the cards from the people you want to contact. You cannot control what they do with your cards, but if you hand them yours, you will get their card in return.

Planned Networking Events: Chamber of Commerce socials are designed with this purpose in mind. Make sure to bring plenty of business cards, know your 30-second commercial, and prepare to offer other information as well. Remember that networking is a two-way street. To get information, you need to give information. Consider volunteering for some of these groups.

Some Ideas for Creating Your Resume

If you were to gather up every "ideal" resume book that has been written over the last year, you could paper-train the world. There is no lack of advice. Resume writing is more art than science, but there are some ideas that seem to be universal among those who help others with resume writing. Try these prompts as you write your resume:

- Be kind to the reader.
- Avoid using career objectives. If you must, make it short, to the point, and focused on the employer's needs. Don't flatter yourself with self-congratulatory language.
- Name, address (optional), email address, phone number(s),
- Consider adding a "QR code," short for Quick Response Code. It is a sort of bar code that can take viewers can scan with a smart phone application in order to view your web site. QR code generators are readily available (Google "QR code") and can be cut and pasted onto your business card or resume. (Try http://www.qrstuff.com/.)
- If a resume is sent digitally (not PDF) you can add URLs that take the viewer to work you have done.
- Use the job description and any notice of the opening to develop key words to imbed in your resume.
- Have a strategy before writing a resume.
- Develop your RABs (results, achievements, benefits) from past work and volunteer experience.
- Think about your ideal job. What would it look like? What is on your resume to prove that you can do your ideal job?

- Tell your story in bullet points. What are your skills and accomplishments? How will they know you can get things done?
- Obstacles you overcame
- Actions used to resolve problems
    - Express the results in qualitative and quantitative terms
    - Use your networks to find an insider
        - Does your resume offer relief for what keeps the hiring manager up at night?
        - Can your contacts ensure that the resume get into the right hands?
- Many cover letters are full of mistakes or miss the point. Precise description of what you offer demonstrates your understanding of the company, and good grammar can carry the day.
- Write a cover letter that is personalized to the hiring manager, if possible, but certainly to the company. Do you understand the company's specific challenges? Prove that you've done your research.
    - Was the company in the news?
    - Anything on its web page you can mention?
    - Have you seen their last quarterly report (publicly held company)?
    - Any speeches, sound bites, etc. from company executives?
    - Have you talked to anyone already employed?
    - Keep it short and simple.
- Avoid gimmicks.
- Google *Wall Street Journal resume*

Accomplishment Statements For Effective Resumes

Amy Jaffe
Career Counselor

Resumes should be accomplishment-driven. They should NOT necessarily focus on duties and responsibilities, but rather on your prospective employer's business needs.

Consider the following questions: What are my professional accomplishments? What am I most proud of? How did I initially become involved? What did I do? How did I do it? What was especially satisfying about doing it? What were the major results or outcomes? (You will want to use a separate sheet and edit it as ideas come to mind.)

The situation:
_____

Your Actions:
_____

The result:
_____

Accomplishment Statement:
_____

_____

The situation:
_____

Your Actions:

The result:

Accomplishment Statement:

The situation:

Your Actions:

The result:

Accomplishment Statement:

Professional Summary For Effective Resumes

Amy Jaffe
Career Counselor

A professional summary gives a concise overview of your accomplishments and experience. It immediately demonstrates your value to the employer by focusing the reader's attention on your most relevant qualifications.

To write your professional summary, follow these steps: (You will want to use a separate sheet and edit it as ideas come to mind.)

1. Describe your current/desired job or profession in a few words:
   _____
   _____
   _____

2. How many years of work experience do you have:
   _____

3. What industries have you worked in:
   _____
   _____
   _____

4. If your education is relevant to your current work, what is your degree: _____

Summarizes answers 1- 4:
_____
_____
_____

5. What are the key skills required of your current or desired job? **Start with a phrase such as *Skilled in* or *Experience with* or *Expert at (Also use action verbs):***

_____

_____

_____

6. What personal qualities, special skills, or exceptional enthusiasms do you offer?

_____

_____

_____

Third sentence summarizes your answer to #6:

_____

_____

_____

7. Pull it all together in a *brief* paragraph of one to three sentences or four or five bulleted statements.

The professional summary quickly establishes your experience, job objective, skills in the specific job function, expertise, and additional technical skills and interpersonal skills. All these should be further demonstrated in the body of your resume.

> Example: *Export/import management professional with over 10 years in international trade and global franchise development. Highly proficient in structuring international joint ventures, quickly evaluating international procurement sources, and financing imports and exports. Comfortable working in different cultural and ethnic environments with multiple language skills.*

_____

_____

_____

Action Verbs for Resumes and Interviews

Accepting _Accepted	_Adopted	_Received
Achieving _Advanced _Attained _Championed	_Accomplished _Earned _Excelled _Promoted	_Achieved _Succeeded _Surpassed _Won
Approving _Approved _Authorized _Awarded	_Certified _Commended _Elected _Nominated	_Recommended _Recognized _Referred _Sponsored
Accounting _Accounted _Audited _Balanced _Budgeted _Calculated _Computed _Credited _Detailed	_Documented _Estimated _Inventoried _Measured _Posted _Reconciled _Recorded _Registered _Reimbursed	_Scanned _Scored _Screened _Selected _Tabulated _Tracked _Validated _Verified
Advising _Advised _Advocated	_Affirmed _Consulted _Counseled	_Helped _Prescribed
Analyzing _Analyzed _Appraised _Ascertained _Assessed _Compared _Considered _Critiqued	_Deciphered _Diagnosed _Evaluated _Examined _Explored _Graded _Impacted _Inspected	_Investigated _Proofed _Proofread _Researched _Reviewed _Studied _Surveyed _Tested
Acquiring _Accrued _Accumulated	_Brought _Acquired _Captured	_Obtained _Recaptured

Assisting	_Enabled	_Supported
_Accommodated	_Served	
_Assisted		
Anticipating	_Forecast	_Predicted
_Anticipated	_Perceived	_Projected
Assembling	_Assembled	_Compiled
_Arranged	_Built	_Constructed
Collecting	_Reclaimed	_Retained
_Collected	_Recouped	_Retrieved
_Intercepted	_Recovered	
Communicating	_Interacted	_Merged
_Communicated	_Interfaced	_Responded
_Dialogued	_Joined	_Translated
_Discussed		
Categorizing	_Departmentalized	_Rated
_Catalogued	_Indexed	_Related
_Categorized	_Logged	_Rendered
_Charted	_Mapped	_Specialized
_Coded	_Ranked	_Specified
_Correlated		
Completing	_Finished	_Provided
_Closed	_Operated	_Submitted
_Completed	_Performed	_Supplied
_Finalized	_Prepared	_Terminated
_Finished	_Processed	_Transacted
_Formalized	_Produced	
Combining	_Compounded	_Linked
_Assimilated	_Included	_Loaded
_Attached	_Incorporated	_Networked
_Collaborated	_Integrated	_Synthesized
_Combined		
Coordinating	_Dealt	-Participated
_Contributed	_Facilitated	-Scheduled
_Cooperated	_Followed	
_Coordinated	_Orchestrated	
Condensing	_Derived	_Reduced
_Concentrated	_Downsized	_Released

_Condensed _Conserved _Consolidated _Cut _Deleted	_Economized _Eliminated _Extracted _Lessened _Narrowed	_Removed _Retired _Saved _Summarized
Delegating _Appointed _Assigned	_Delegated _Designated _Devoted	_Issued _Notified _Required
Creating _Conceived _Conceptualized _Configured _Created _designed _Developed _Devised _Engineered	_Established _Fabricated _Formed _Formulated _Founded _Generated _Innovated _Installed	_Invented _Modeled _Molded _Originated _Programmed _Rendered _Styled _Visualized
Emphasizing _Emphasizing	_Focused	_Underscored
Expanding _Deregulated _Diversified	_Divested _Enlarged _Expanded _Extended	_Grew _Increased _Multiplied _Syndicated
Explaining _Clarified	_Defined _Described	_Elaborated _Illustrated
Marketing _Advertised _Brokered _Merchandised _Penetrated	_Displayed _Exhibited _Lobbied _Marketed	_Positioned _Publicized _Sold _Solicited
Instituting _Introduced _Launched _Opened _Piloted	_Pioneered _Raised _Reignited _Reinvented	_Set up _Sparked _Spearheaded _Started
Negotiating _Agreed	_Confronted _Contracted	_Proposed _Reasoned

| _Arbitrated
_Challenged
_Conciliated
_Concurred | _Mediated
_Negotiated | _Renegotiated
_Subcontracted |
|---|---|---|
| **Finding**
_Located | _Sought
_Sourced | _Traced |
| **Guaranteeing**
_Ensured | _Guaranteed | _Insured |
| **Impacting**
_Affected | _Effected | _Impacted |
| **Maximizing**
_Capitalized | _Maximized | _Optimized |
| **Using**
_Exploited | _Used | _Utilized |
| **Hiring**
_Employed
_Enlisted | _Hired
_Interviewed
_Recruited | _Rehired
_Restaffed
-Staffed |
| **Identifying**
_Decided
_Detected | _Determined
_Discovered | _Identified
_Pinpointed |
| **Implementing**
_Activated
_Actualized | _Administered
_Applied
_Executed | _Implemented
_Initialized
-Initiated |
| **Motivating**
_Convinced
_Encouraged
_Entertained | _Influenced
_Inspired
_Interested
_Involved | _Motivated
_Persuaded |
| **Moving**
_Drove
_Emerged
_Moved | _Navigated
_Placed
_Pushed | _Relocated
_Returned
_Transitioned |
| **Organizing**
_Grouped
_Organized | _Planned
_Prioritized
_Sorted | _Strategized
_Structured |
| **Preventing**
_Circumvented
_Deferred | _Deflected
_Diverted
_Preempted | _Prevented
_Thwarted |

Solving	_Resolved	_Troubleshot
_Neutralized	_Treated	_Turned
Speaking	_Moderated	_Quoted
_Addressed	_Narrated	_Reported
_Announced	_Presented	_Spoke
Strengthening	_Transformed	_Upgraded
_Systematized	_Updated	_Vitalized
Understanding	_Interpreted	_Practiced
_Construed	_Learned	_Realized
_Familiarized	_Mastered	
Writing	_Corresponded	_Published
_Authored	_Drafted	_Rewrote
_Coauthored	_Drew up	_Transcribed
_Composed	_Edited	_Wrote
Teaching	_Enlightened	_Mentored
_Coached	_Illustrated	_Proved
_Cross-trained	_Indoctrinated	_Retrained
_Debriefed	_Informed	_Showed
_Demonstrated	_Instructed	_Taught
_Disproved	_Lectured	_Trained
_Educated		
Purchasing	_Funded	_Procured
_Bid	_Invested	_Purchased
_Bought	_Leased	_Requisitioned
_Collateralized	_Ordered	
Sending	_Dispersed	_Outsourced
_Delivered	_Distributed	_Routed
_Dispatched	_Exported	_Transferred
_Dispensed	_Forwarded	_Transmitted
Improving	_Normalized	_Re-sequenced
_Accelerated	_Overhauled	_Reshaped
_Adapted	_Perfected	_Restored
_Adjusted	_Progressed	_Restructured
_Altered	_Realigned	_Retooled
_Augmented	_Rebuilt	_Returned
_Automated	_Reconstructed	_Revamped
_Centralized	_Recreated	_Revised

_Changed	_Rectified	_Revitalized
_Converted	_Recycled	_Rewired
_Corrected	_Redesigned	_Shaped
_Debugged	_Reengineered	_Simplified
_Energized	_Reinforced	_Solidified
_Enhanced	_Remodeled	_Solved
_Exchanged	_Renewed	_Stabilized
_Expedited	_Reorganized	_Standardized
_Improved	_Repaired	_Stimulated
_Modernized	_Replaced	_Streamed
_Modified	_Replenished	
Managing	_Enforced	_Monitored
_Acted	_Exercised	_Oversaw
_Allocated	_Governed	_Presided
_Assumed	_Guided	_Protected
_Chaired	_Handled	_Regulated
_Co managed	_Held	_Represented
_Commanded	_Led	_Supervised
_Conducted	_Maintained	_Sustained
_Controlled	_Managed	
_Directed	_Manipulated	

Interviewing Skills

Preparing for the Interview

- Write down your top 10-15 characteristics, skills, and experience levels that you want the employer to know about you.
- Determine if your list is consistent with what the employer is looking for; if not, revise as necessary.
- Get a copy of the job description if possible from the HR office.
- Research the company's website to learn as much as you can about it.
- Locate friends/associates who know something about the company to learn the inside scoop.
- Write down a list of questions for the interviewer.
- Arrive early; it is a good idea to do a dry run by checking out the location ahead of time.
- Wear appropriate clothing and be ready for a lunch or group interview.
- Come prepared with enough resumes and other documents for everyone on the interview team.
- Use resources such as Internet sites.

Researching the Company

Researching the company serves many purposes. First, it gives you information about mission, products, business structure, initiatives, and biographies of certain employees. Second, it gives you enough information to ask focused questions to sound knowledgeable about the business and its industry. Third, it shows you are interested enough to do your homework.

Look at the company website for information on its business, products/services and personnel. Use the links on the website to find out more about the industry and any professional associations they link to. Also research competitors and how others view the company.

If you are applying for a different position at the same company you currently work for, you still need to do your research. Get a copy of the job description, talk with people in that department, and learn about issues they face as well as skills required to do the job.

find something in your research to bring up in conversation when you make contact. Example: In reading the bios on the company website, you learn one of the people interviewing you is a sailor and owns a Friendship Sloop.

Write your answers to the following questions:

- What impresses you about this company?
- Why do you want to work for this company? List specific criteria that make you a good match for this company.
- What evidence do you have that they are a good fit for you? What do you know about how the company operates and the requirements of the job, and how do your education and experience match up?
- What do you know about the issues facing this company?

Net Links:

www.fastcompany.com
www.ValueLine.com
www.rileyguide.com
www.corporateinformation.com
www.hooversonline.com

What Prospective Employers Want to Know About You

Four Basic Questions
1. Can you do the job?
2. What are you like?

3. Will you be part of the problem or part of the solution?
4. How much will you cost?

Questions interviewers use to get answers to the four basic questions:

- How do you react when you realize you made a mistake?
- How would you describe your last boss?
- What did you like most and least in your last job?
- How did you justify your salary in your last job?
- Are you sure you have the qualifications for this job?
- What interests you most about this job?
- Which of your achievements gave you the greatest satisfaction?
- Why do you want to work for us?
- What part of your work experience prepared you for this job?
- When you have had problems on the job, how did you react?
- When are you the most confident?
- What were your most important accomplishments?
- Describe your experience managing others.
- Describe yourself (in other words, will we be able to get along with you?).
- Why did you leave your last job?
- What would you like to avoid in your next job?
- What is your professional goal?

- What do you look for in a company?
- What are you are looking for in your next job?
- Can you give me examples of jobs that you liked?
- What are your strong points?
- What did you like about your last job?
- How do you measure success on the job?
- Where do you need improvement?
- Do you have a long-term career objective?
- Describe yourself as a leader.
- What were the results of your most recent performance review?
- What do need to learn next to take your career where you want it go?
- What kind of writing and speaking have you done?

Promising Future's Axioms for Salary Negotiations

Most of us are uncomfortable talking about money. Our reluctance grows as we realize that we want to emphasize how our unique talents can help the employer, and not focus on what we want from the company. These tips will help emphasize what you offer while you get the salary you deserve.

Axiom #1: Do Your Homework

Complete your thoughts about what you need from the employer:

What motivates you?
- Intrinsic process – motivated by fun
- Instrumental – motivated by rewards
- Self-concept external – motivated by reputation
- Self-concept internal – motivated by challenge
- Goal internalized – motivated by the cause

How much do you need to earn?
- "Survival" means what to you?
- What does your current standard of living cost?
- What do other people in similar positions earn?

What do your accomplishments demonstrate about how much you can help a company succeed?
- Express worth in terms of 'A-Bs' (What did you Achieve and what were the Benefits that reflect their challenges?)
- Accomplishments weigh more than experience. What have you accomplished that shows you can help, stressing achievements that reflect their needs. Be ready to quantify your accomplishments.

Research the company:

What do you know about the salary culture of the company you are courting?
- How often are salaries reviewed?
- What benefits are offered?
- Is there an incentive or profit-sharing program?
- How stable is the position?

What does the position require of you?
- Will you have additional responsibilities that require more?
- How steep is the learning curve for your new position?
- What do they need to have done to bring success to past employers that will transfer to your new employer?

Sites for researching salary information:

www.careerjournal.com/salaries/index.html

www.careerjournal.com/salaries/calculator/index.html
Helps calculate the cost of living among different cities in the United States.

www.jobstar.org/tools/salary/sal-surv.htm
Salary information

Axiom #2: Avoid Talking About Salary Too Soon and Avoid Giving Actual Figures

Discussions about money should occur late in the hiring process and should be brought up by the interviewer. You want to spend your time emphasizing what you bring, not what you will receive. If pressed, offer that your salary requirements are negotiable and that you will know them better once you see that there is a fit between your career goals and the company's needs.

If pushed again, ask for a range. If pushed even further, cite your research results: "I understand a position of this nature pays (insert your number here)." If they ask about your past earnings, remember: You are not applying for the job you want to leave.

Recall two of the keys to career success:

First, you are not looking for a job: *You are there to help them solve problems.*

Second, you are always moving to something—helping the company succeed: *Try to avoid discussing your current compensation for as long as possible. When you do talk about it, discuss total compensation. Gather this information from both your current or most recent compensation package and, if possible, from the company you want to work for.*

Axiom #3: Determine the "Sweet Spot" and Optimize, Not Maximize

Compare what the employer wants to accomplish to what you need:

What keeps them up at night?
What gets them out of bed in the morning?
What keeps you up at night?
What gets you out of bed in the morning?

You will be working with these people every day, so be fair. You do not want to start your new job feeling undervalued, and they don't want you to start wondering how you will ever justify the high salary.

Focus on your goals, not on putting something over on anyone. You don't want to create hard feelings. Make sure what you are asking for reflects what you can actually do. Keep in mind, however, that future compensation depends upon what happens now.

The best job isn't always the one that pays the most, so prioritize your job-related values

Axiom #4: Use Uncertainty to Your Advantage

You are about to form a partnership. They want you, and the job sounds attractive. You can benefit from the fact that they don't know what you will accept for a salary. Let them do the talking. Keep in mind that you are looking for the "sweet spot."

Creating a Business Card

A business card is an essential tool for a job search. Networking opportunities as well as informational and formal interviews are a great time to practice using this tool. It puts your name and contact information in someone else's hands, and gives you an opening to request a card from someone else for future reference.

For those used to carrying a card from an employer, having a card to pull out will feel very familiar. It will be new having a card that is just about you. If you have recently been laid off, it may be tempting to use the old card from your last employer. But it does not offer your current contact information, and it may be misleading regarding your employment situation.

What to include on your card:

- Your name and company name (if applicable)
- Your address (if you are not comfortable giving this out, you don't have to); some people purchase a PO Box to use during a job search
- A title or brief description of your area of expertise
- Phone numbers, including or limited to your cell phone, if this is how you prefer to be contacted
- Fax number if you have one
- Website address if you have one
- Email address

- Bulleted areas of expertise.
- If you are launching a new business, this is an opportunity to create a logo. Your logo and the color and card stock help create a recognizable look and will help your card stand out.

On the Front – easy to understand contact information

Jane Smith, *Distribution Specialist*

P.O. Box 555, Nowhere, USA 00000

Ph: 207-555-8899

Cell: 215-5555

Fax: 207-555-1122

Website: www.lookatme.biz

Email: jsmith@lookatme.com

Please connect with me on LinkedIn

On the Back —highlighted accomplishments

- 10 years of distribution experience in the food industry
- MBA w/concentration in distribution technology
- Fluent in Spanish, French, and Italian
- Five years of experience in the international food market

Stages of Change
Often Encountered by Workers Making an
Unplanned Career Change

Many authors, such as Nancy Schlossberg, Elizabeth Kubler-Ross and Hopson and Adams have written about stages of change. They imply that the process of unexpected change follows a rigidly defined and predictable sequence which is not their intent. Rather, your experiences may follow this path or you may have a different experience. Over the years my clients have tended to follow the stages listed below, but not always. Looking at these can help you tune your scanner to your day to day experiences and help you develop some strategies for easing what might be a difficult time.

Disbelief generally comes first. Workers I have met have said things such as,

> "They're always doing this. I can wait them out until they call me back."
> "This is just a phase to make the books look good."
> "My job is essential. I won't be touched."
> "It's my age."

If you find yourself murmuring similar phrases, a reality check might help, but it may also be painful. We draw a good deal of our sense of worth then belonging from the work we do and losing our job is, at the least, unpleasant. Allow yourself some time to adjust and look and share your concerns with family and friends. Stiff upper lips are fine, but also look for a suitable release mechanism, such as I offer in the *Momentum* section.

Betrayal:
        a. "I have been here 15 years and this is the thanks I get?"

2. Confusion:
   a. "I'm 43 years old. What will I do now?"
   b. "I suppose I should swallow my pride and go see the counselor."

3. Anger:
   a. "Wait until they need something and I'm not there!"

4. Resolution:
   a. "Free at last, free at last!"
   b. "It's not about me, and there's more to my life than my job. Time to start networking."

After the Interview: Thank You Note Examples

Date:

Name:
Title:
Address:

Dear Mr./Ms. (last name):

Thank you for taking the time to meet with me on (*date*) to discuss the (*position title*) you have available. I appreciate the opportunity to learn more about (*company name*) and to discuss how my qualifications can meet your needs.

I would like to become part of your team and feel strongly I can be an asset to (*company name*). My experience in (*type of experience*) plus my training (*refer to training*) will enable me to be a strong contributing member of your (*name of team*) organization. I look forward to hearing from you.

Please let me know if there is any information I can provide that will help you in the decision-making process. If I don't hear from you, I will call you next (*day*), as you suggested. Thank you for your time and consideration.

Sincerely,

Date

Mrs. Important Business
Human Resources Manager
ABC Company
Address

Dear Mrs. Business:

Thank you for your hospitality during my visit to XYZ Company. My discussion with you was both enlightening and encouraging.

I am confident that I am an excellent candidate for the Quality Assurance Auditor position at XYZ. My diverse accounting background, along with my broad-based experience in the automotive industry, will help me make a positive contribution to your team.

I am excited about the position, and I look forward to working with you and your team if given the opportunity.

Thank you again for your time and consideration. I look forward to speaking with you soon. .

Sincerely,

A word about LinkedIn and Facebook

It is pointless to go into too much detail here, as both sites change and grow. Networking is the key, and LinkedIn and Facebook will help keep your networks alive and vibrant.

Keep your pages professional. Do not put anything on these pages that you do not want an employer to see (they will look). Like your resume, your pages are marketing pieces. They share the same information that comes on your resume, even if they are not a resume.
Judi Jones, of Infoharbor, advises that you make your profile interesting, and not just informative. You can develop interest via:

- Interesting (but accurate) titles
- Accomplishment statements (that you can support)
- Pictures
- Recommendations
- Endorsements

Be certain to include keywords that an employer might use to scan your skills. Include links to other sites such as your website, Twitter, Facebook, etc. Make sure your summary answers the questions:

- Why should someone care about you?
- What solution are you providing?
- What do you have to offer?
- Where are the key words for specialties?

Third party recommendations carry weight, so use them. When you ask for recommendations, cite your projects and include your resume.

You can include content such as case studies (remember confidentiality), slideshows, or videos. You might even want a blog to set yourself up as a thought leader.

You will start getting opportunities to do thank you notes and congratulatory messages, but make them personal. Don't settle for the boilerplate offered by the site. Establish a short dialogue with anyone who wants to link with you.
Pursue my LinkedIn site for examples.

Appendices

Applying the Science of Chaos to Managing Your Career, or Why You Can Organize Serendipity

In this section I explore the ideas from physics and meteorology that have shaped my thinking about career development. I believe you will be encouraged if you understand the thinking behind the exercises.

I experienced a chaotic moment in 1988 when I finished my doctoral work examining the career development of female college professors. My research disproved everything I had held dear about the growth of an individual's career self-concept. I previously believed that linear, cause and effect-based developmental models offered a clear map for career growth and change. Understanding those models could help counselors predict the issues typically occurring at any age. Once we identified those developmental issues, we could plan neat little interventions. The work of Levinson outlined in *The Seasons of a Man's Life* was especially enchanting.

But there was a hitch. Levinson and others primarily focused on the development of men. For my dissertation, I interviewed women to see how career stages might neatly unfold over time for the other half of the work force. The age-related stage models came apart like a cheap potato chip in cold dip. The linear career models I cherished quickly unraveled. Something was missing with developmental theory and I was frustrated. How can we better understand the formative influences on career self-concept?

Serendipity led me to a Nova special on the *New Science of Chaos* broadcast in 1989. The presenters reviewed the emerging concepts of chaos theory and developed a new vocabulary for describing how systems gain complexity. One startling assertion struck me: Chaos generates order. When our careers seem to careen into a chaotic state it is hard to believe any order can come from the painful turbulence. Yes, losing a job may hurt, but chaos theory offers hope. Understanding the order generating power of chaos started with trying to predict the weather.

The quintessential example of chaos and system building emerged in meteorology by using computers to solve the ancient dilemma, "What will the weather be like tomorrow?" The Nova program portrayed Edward Lorenz's struggle to build a linear computer model that could predict the weather. He programmed such variables as heat and the speed of convection currents into his computer and began producing the weather models.

He then re-ran his program, rounding the numbers of his initial variables. Instead of a perfect copy of his first run, his second set of results offered a completely different version of the weather. The small differences in his initial conditions gave him dramatically different results -- and chaos theory was born.

Sensitivity to Initial Conditions and Feedback

Predicting career outcomes and predicting the weather present major difficulties. Lorenz believed that he could build computer models that would accurately predict the weather into infinity, if only he had enough data and could control all the variables. He came to the disappointing conclusion that the sensitivity to initial conditions was so great that any disruption could enter a feedback cycle, like a squeal through a microphone that grows from a little hum into a crescendo. At first the computer program would produce a sunny day. With a minor alteration the program would produce a tornado. Lorenz concluded that, given the right conditions, a butterfly flapping its wings in China could cause a tornado in Texas.

Our careers can face disruptions from Lorenz's butterflies as well. We never can predict when our career self-concepts will face information that no longer fits our career beliefs. If we encounter a piece of information that leads us to question our beliefs, it's like hearing two tones at the same time that do not sound good together. That's called dissonance. Imagine a group of elementary school students coming together for the first time, attempting to tune their new, untried violins. Dogs will howl and cats will run for cover. Our startled pets are experiencing the sound of dissonance.

When our career beliefs are threatened a new kind of dissonance roars in our consciousness and we must readjust our view of the world. We never know what piece of career dissonance will result in a crescendo in our career "weather." Other writers have called the random chance that dissonance can enter a feedback cycle and create a reaction all out of proportion to the stimulus "dissonance roulette."

Dissonance roulette occurs without warning. One fellow in one of my workshops became my poster child for that unexpected tipping point. A group of adults meeting with me had been out of work for some time and they were worried. As we introduced ourselves one fellow seemed especially unresponsive. He sat there with his chin on his hands, staring straight ahead, participating with monosyllabic grunts. I was helpless to engage him as he filled all of us with uneasy visions of a disgruntled worker about to go berserk. At the end of the first day's session he bolted from the room to the relief of all present.

I returned to the facility the next day and carried my first load of materials to our dark and isolated conference room. I detected movement by the window and was startled to see our glowering participant emerge from the shadows and approach with his hand outstretched. I didn't know what to do or say. "I have a three-page hand-out and I'm not afraid to use it," came to mind but it did not seem sufficient for the danger I perceived. He grabbed my hand and began to pump it vigorously; thanking me profusely for all the help I'd given him the previous day. "Listening to you made everything click and now I'm excited and ready to get started on a new career." I congratulated him on his sudden epiphany as my pulse began to return to normal.

Complex Adaptive Systems

Chaos theory helps explain how complex adaptive systems, such as weather or our career self-concepts, behave. Complex adaptive systems are all around us. Any time elements come together for their common good, you have a system. The economy is a system; a nail rusting in the dirt is system. Our bodies are made up of multiple systems. Our career self-concepts are complex adaptive systems, constantly acquiring information about their environment and their interaction with the environment. As our career self-concept acquire new information, it adjusts and adapts.

Like other complex adaptive systems, our career self-concepts identify regularities in order to create models for future behaviors. Systems consequently behave according to the models that they have created. Over time, the models that the systems create compete with each other. We can never predict what the system will do at any distant point in the future, like predicting the weather, but we can predict tendencies toward specific behavior.

Many have tried to find easy matches between the systems I call "career self-concept" to the system made up of all the jobs we might pursue. Most of us have taken inventories to tell us which jobs we might enjoy. Commonly used assessments generate a three-letter score that is compared to a list of occupations. The three-letter scores were developed as the result of the work of John Holland and others to simplify the job search process. Holland believed people gravitate toward certain job families based on their personality. Career inventories like the *Self-Directed Search* or the *Career Decision Making System* help us understand how we seek the work environments that suit our personalities. Two organic systems, the jobs available in the work environment and our career self-concept, adapt to or reject each other.

We start with a genetic predisposition to certain behaviors and then learn to adapt to our environment as we grow. Individual learning experiences shape our beliefs, and those beliefs shape the way we react to future experiences. As we do so, we build a complex system of opinions about what works for us. Some serve us well, and some are superstitions that see a cause-and-effect relationship where there is none. As we lumber through our daily chores our career self-concept, as a self-adaptive system, gains complexity, shaping and refining our belief system.

Within the structure of our self-adaptive belief system dwells its triumph and its doom. As long as the system can tolerate small waves of dissonance, the system moves along. We cannot predict, however (like the pensive worker I described above), when some dissonant information will go beyond what the system can bear, and then it collapses into chaos, dissipating to form a new set of career beliefs. Workers who have toiled at the same job for many years, only to have the plant close on both their job and their work identity, can understand what that feels like.

The Role of Intuition

Our tendencies toward specific behaviors are faster than rational thought will allow, which leads to intuition. Intuition is our way of sorting through a huge amount of cognitive experiences and creating patterns, the easiest way we have to organize all we have learned. We develop intuition by analyzing our cognitive experiences. Analysis builds intuition and intuition leads us to further analysis.

In other words, analysis is too cumbersome for most career decisions, yet we rely on analysis to allow our intuition to work effectively. The more we learn, the more we empower our intuition, or our capacity to identify patterns. Yes, intuition may be viewed as the opposite of analysis, but actually intuition is the result of building a repertoire of patterns through the analytic experience. Systems grow by analyzing their experiences, gathering data, building a set of patterns, and learning intuition. We use our intuition to gather and respond to the information that adds complexity to our career self-concepts.

If we accept that career self-concept is a complex adaptive system that can be observed and shaped, chaos theory offers support and direction for shaping our career. That theory allows us to better understand the dynamics of system growth and change. Career counseling can provide the cognitive dissonance that allows the career self-concept as a system to add complexity to its structure.

Chaos theory, ironically, may not be the best term to describe the career chaos that the theory is attempting to understand. Chaos implies a totally non-deterministic set of events without any relationship to one another. We simply cannot operate with a totally random system. Without the patterns chaos generates, the way we execute our daily tasks would have no order at all, and bear no relationship to our skills, values, or environmental preferences. We would simply stumble about in a random fashion, walking into the furniture, assuming that we moved at all.

By reflecting on your career so far you can bring what you learn to sculpt the future. While our work may seem random at times, we are bound by the intuitive process that recognizes the patterns we tend to repeat themselves. We tend to enjoy the same sorts of successes, and we tend to repeat the same mistakes. The elements of our behaviors and the way we practice using our preferred skills, for example, clusters together within a rather narrow set of repetitive patterns throughout our day and throughout our careers. Our career behaviors exhibit characteristics of chaos because the ways we apply our skills (and the skills we use) are connected, and future applications are difficult to predict in any detail. We must content ourselves with understanding our tendency to repeat favored behaviors.

The Language of Chaos: Sensitivity to Initial Conditions and Feedback

The concept of the random application of our skills and the "dissonance roulette" that shapes our career self-concept is known to chaos theorists as sensitivity to initial conditions and feedback. We do not know how the particular application of skills will be applied, what will come along to influence our behavior, or how beliefs will influence future career actions. The complexities of the actual application are so overwhelming that they totally defy prediction. They appear chaotic.

Strange Attractor

Over time, work behaviors take on patterns that can be observed. Career planning requires mastering the art of predicting preferred career tendencies. Where will the tendencies take us and which tendencies tend to lead to success?

Patterns usually form around one or two central points called strange attractors. It is as though our behaviors were gathered by some sort of magnetic field or central point that drew us within its orbit. You may not know what you will be doing tomorrow at 3 p.m., but if you step back and observe your behaviors from an adequate distance, chaos will fade and your afternoons tend to follow a pattern. Over time, these patterns take on a gyroscopic tendency to form a stability of their own.

The patterns that make up our career self-concept may form very early in our development, where they may be a bit difficult to detect. I encountered an individual who exemplifies early establishment of the strange attractors that seem to guide our behaviors. He was a volunteer guide aboard the World War II submarine *USS Requin,* exhibited at the Carnegie Science Center in Pittsburgh. He volunteered on the *Requin* after retiring from a career in electronics. The submarine represented only one stage in his pursuit of anything with an electrical circuit. As we chatted, he reminisced about his boyhood interest in ham radios. He gazed pensively into the distance and remarked, "The patterns were there, even then."

Bifurcation

Our career self-concept, however, is a system nested within other systems. We work within organizations that interact with other organizations. The organizations self-organize within an economy that is itself nested within a social system. Within this web, we are influenced by the interaction of the initial set of conditions that formed the basic set of assumptions we hold about our preferred work behaviors and the world where we practice these behaviors. As we orbit merrily about our strange attractors, we are gathering information. At certain, unpredictable points in our orbits we experience a degree of cognitive dissonance that defies integration into our career beliefs. In most instances we absorb the new experience within the framework of our existing way of doing things, and our self- concept wobbles a bit before it trundles on.

In extreme instances, we experience a bifurcation point or tear in the fabric of our system that leads us to reorganize or add complexity to our system, and create new patterns of behavior. Bifurcations might occur from major events, such as a job change. They also occur when a random piece of information, like the straw that menaced the proverbial camel, precipitates change beyond what one would expect. These changes seem random and unpredictable, based on the sensitivity to the initial conditions that formed our self-concept. The influence may come from something someone says in passing. The casual comment resonates with other pieces of information that had been fermenting in the backs of our minds, precipitating a reaction all out of proportion to the stimulus.

I encountered a physician who had lost his license and needed a new career direction. He certainly experienced a bifurcation as his personal and professional identity as a doctor was ripped asunder. He also planned to move to another state for a new start, further complicating the adjustment process. He was faced with the challenge of creating an entirely new identity.

Fractals: Self-Similar Scaling

Scaling is a concept used to describe fractals. As systems interact and their systems gain complexity, they acquire the characteristics of fractals. Fractals are shapes formed when the same shape is repeated on both larger and smaller scales. As the patterns repeat themselves, the overall shape is repeated in the details.

Our lungs are fractals, exhibiting the self-similar shapes of the alveoli. The alveoli are the part of the respiratory system where the primary gas exchange occurs in the lungs. Repeating these tiny, self-similar shapes allows us an extensive surface area for absorbing oxygen contained in a relatively small area.

Our career self-concepts display the fractals characteristics of self-similar shaping as our daily behaviors patterns repeat themselves in various permutations until they make up our careers. The skills, such as reading, writing, manipulating objects, and speaking, we employ in our daily activity are actually not that extensive. When we practice these skills and abilities, however, they become very complex as we solve the problems we face each day. Doing so reflects the problems our employee organizations encounter within the general economic environments where our employers do their business. Our careers are the sum total of repeating smaller patterns. From a Meta perspective, we need to keep a close eye on the greater environment as our daily tasks will reflect the greater economy.

Chaos and Careers

The weather is so sensitive to its initial conditions that one tiny disruption, like a tipping point, can create huge consequences. Hence, the flapping of butterfly's wings in China can cause a cyclone in Texas. Given the likelihood that some butterfly is flapping its wings somewhere, butterflies could represent a terrible menace, but only the exact right conditions can result in such catastrophic consequences, all out of proportion to the initial "flap." During our search for self-awareness, a great deal of effort can go into creating the constructive dissonance needed to bring real change in our career behaviors, previously described as dissonance roulette. We can never know just when change will occur, but if we persist, change will occur.

Strange attractors explain how a few basic career beliefs can shape a set of complex and repeating career behaviors. John Holland's iconic six individual personality types, listed in the following table, represent a very basic summary of skill preferences.

Investigative or Scientific:
Characterized by an interest in understanding the physical world, prefers independence, likes to approach problems regionally, and enjoys science.
Artistic:
Prefers self-expression and original thought and creativity, avoids structure, and needs individual expression.

Social:
Enjoys attention and self-expression social and outgoing, solves problems through discussion, and likes to lead.
Enterprising or Business:
Good with words, enthusiastic and adventurous, self-confident and assertive, and likes to persuade others.
Conventional or Office Operations:
Stable and dependable, organized and efficient, don't mind rules and regulations.
Realistic or Crafts:
Practical, like to work outdoors, enjoys building and repairing things.

They can be combined and reiterated to form the matrix of all career behaviors. A carpenter might identify *Realistic,* as her first preference, but might also include the descriptors in *Enterprising,* and *Investigative* to describe herself as a carpenter in business for herself. These few descriptors combine to form all of her complex career patterns. If she leans toward working for someone else and on a team, *Social* might replace *Enterprising*.

Our career behaviors orbit about the strange attractor, generating similar, yet unique career preferences, among all the people who have careers. Many individuals might exhibit similar combinations of Holland's six personality types, yet show preference for very different behaviors. Each individual, however, will show repeating behavioral tendencies in his or her career cycle. This presence of the attractor allows us to predict future sources of satisfaction by identifying past behavior patterns, much like our electronics enthusiast on the *Requin*.

Still, the presence of the strange attractors does not prevent systems from gaining complexity or dissipating and then reforming. Bifurcations occur in chaotic systems as the attractor takes on new direction and forms. For career "attractors," bifurcations and the subsequent shift in behavior can result from unexpected or planned career change, such as lay-offs, past aspirations that may come back to haunt us, or emerging new interests.

If our carpenter was injured and could no longer work as a carpenter, then she may look to her lesser preferences and use *Realistic* and *Enterprising* preferences to work in a hardware store, or a *Social* preference to teach carpentry to others. If her experience and interests in management open other doors, she might go into construction management, as area she might not have predicted when she started her career. Some bit of experience created the cognitive dissonance needed to begin a quest for areas related to her initial interest in carpentry.

The application of systems thinking and chaos theory to career development helps to explain how behavior patterns, repeated over time, gain complexity and form careers. It also offers a blueprint for interventions that can help reshape the self-adaptive process. If you believe you can sculpt a new career self-concept, then you can hope to find a process for success. The turbulence of career change that we experience will generate patterns. When we learn to nurture the turbulence that seems to govern our careers, we can organize serendipity.

Re-Careering After 50: Organizing Serendipity for Those with Lots of Experience

If you are either a Baby Boomer (50 to 65) or passing the traditional retirement age, it can become a time of growth and adventure. (If you have not yet reached 50, but you expect to someday, the material that follows will still be very useful.) It can also be a time to explore new interests. You are at the crossroads between being at the peak of your skills (and expensive to employers) and facing age discrimination.

We are living in uncertain times. The dollar continues to lose buying power while Social Security and pensions, if they are available, do not keep up, especially with rising health care costs. Our political process offers little hope for alleviating economic problems confronting aging Boomers. Fear that we will live beyond our financial security leaves us wanting to do something about our futures.

Why are you re-careering? You have valuable skills. You expect to live and work longer than your parents did and you are not ready to retire. You still want a sense of purpose and acknowledgement. You may also need the money. The material in this book will help you develop self-descriptors to focus on your job search strategy and what you have to sell future customers and employers.

I offer three ideas that will help you tune your scanner and enhance self-awareness. First, people over 50 bring a useful perspective to organizations, and second, a set of powerful "SCAN skills," such as speaking, listening, reading, writing, and mathematics. Finally, many folks who re-career after 50 begin their own enterprises, and you could well be one of them.

Skill and Maturity Awareness

Your mastery of SCANS skills will help you articulate the sorts of problems you can solve for future employers and focus on the skills you want to employ. In my career as an educator I learned to maintain control while 500 adolescents ate lunch. I was good at it. I don't want to do it again, so it's not a skill I intend to market. Review this list below to identify your favorite skills while avoiding those you prefer not to practice in the future.

As part of your scanner tuning process, review these skills. As you will see, they are basic to all industries in varying degrees. Reviewing these skills will tune your scanner to the skills you can "sell," and build some language to use on resumes, in cover letters, and during interviews. Pay special attention to gathering anecdotes you can use to prove your competencies.

SCANS Skills (Adapted from *What Work Requires of Schools* -- The Secretary's Commission on Achieving Necessary Skills (SCANS))		I want to use this
Basic Skills: Reads, writes, performs arithmetic and mathematical operations, listens, and speaks		
Speaking	Organizes ideas and communicates orally	
Listening	Receives, attends to, interprets, and responds to verbal messages and other cues	
Reading	Locates, understands, and interprets written information in prose and in documents such as manuals, graphs, and schedules	
Writing	Communicates thoughts,	

		ideas, information, and messages in writing; and creates documents such as letters, directions, manuals, reports, graphs, and flow charts	
	Mathematics	Performs basic computations and approaches practical problems by choosing appropriately from a variety of mathematical techniques	

Thinking Skills: Thinks creatively, makes decisions, solves problems, visualizes, knows how to learn, and reasons

	Creative Thinking	generates new ideas	
	Decision Making	specifies goals and constraints, generates alternatives, considers risks, and evaluates and chooses best alternative	
	Identify and Solve Problems	recognizes problems and devises and implements plan of action	
	Seeing Things in the Mind's Eye	organizes and processes symbols, pictures, graphs, objects, and other information	
	Knowing How to Learn	uses efficient learning techniques to acquire and apply new knowledge and skills	
	Reasoning	discovers a rule or	

	principle underlying the relationship between two or more <<<right?>>>objects and applies it when solving a problem	
Personal Qualities: Displays responsibility, self-esteem, sociability, self-management, and integrity and honesty			
Responsibility	Exerts a high level of effort and perseveres towards goal attainment	
Self-Esteem	Believes in own self-worth and maintains a positive view of self	
Sociability	Demonstrates understanding, friendliness, adaptability, empathy, and	
Self-Management	Assesses self accurately, sets personal goals, monitors progress, and exhibits self-control	
Integrity, Honesty, and Confidentiality	Chooses ethical courses of action	
Resources: Identifies, organizes, plans, and allocates resources			
Manages Time	Selects goal-relevant activities, ranks them, allocates time, and prepares and follows schedules	
Manages Money	Uses or prepares	

		budgets, makes forecasts, keeps records, and makes adjustments to meet objectives	
	Material and Facilities	Acquires, stores, allocates, and uses materials or space efficiently	
	Human Resources	Assesses skills and distributes work accordingly, evaluates performance and provides feedback	
Interpersonal: Works with others			
	Participates as Member of a Team	contributes to group effort, teaches others new skills	
	Serves Clients/Customers	works to satisfy customers' expectations	
	Exercises Leadership	communicates ideas to justify position, persuades and convinces others, responsibly challenges existing procedures and policies	
	Negotiates	works toward agreements involving exchange of resources, resolves divergent interests	
	Works with Diversity	works well with men and women from diverse backgrounds	

Information: Acquires and uses information		
Interprets and Communicates Information		
Acquires and Evaluates Information		
Organizes and Maintains Information Uses Computers to Process Information		
Systems: Understands complex inter-relationships		
Understands Systems	Knows how social, organizational, and technological systems work and operates effectively with them	
Monitors and Corrects Performance	Distinguishes trends, predicts impacts on systems operations, diagnoses deviations in systems' performance, and corrects malfunctions	
Improves or Designs Systems	Suggests modifications to existing systems and develops new or alternative systems to improve performance	
Technology: Works with a variety of technologies		
Selecting Tools and Procedures	chooses procedures, tools or equipment, including computers and related technologies	

Applying Technology to Task	Understands overall intent and proper procedures for setup and operation of equipment
Maintains and Troubleshoots Equipment	Prevents, identifies, or solves problems with equipment, including computers and other technologies

Now take stock and celebrate all you have learned. Once more, let's review those skills. How would you rate yourself in the areas I list below?

Areas of Experience and Maturity	I will develop	I can hold my own	I am confident
Read and understand work related material			
Acquire, evaluate, and integrate new information.			
Listening and reflection			
Use, adapt, and communicate thoughts and ideas by writing and speaking			
Understand and utilize the technology you encounter			
Understand and apply the mathematics required by your areas of interest			
Self-directed learning – teaching yourself			
Solve problems and design action plans			

Understand pictures and graphs			
Possess self-esteem and self-efficacy			
Take personal responsibility and take initiative			
Manage your emotions under duress			
Set goals and manage your time in order to reach them			
Organize plans and allocate resources (time, money, staff, etc.)			
Teach, mentor, and coach others			
Identify and deliver customer's expectations			
Persuade and convince others, such as leadership and sales			
Work with a diverse group of colleagues			
Negotiate agreements and resolve divergent interests			
Describe your special, preferred skills in your own words			

Your current and future work experiences include working with people from the very young to the very old. Any description of a particular age group allows you to reflect on the similarities and differences. Tune your scanner to watch for those characteristics that strengthen your effort to re-career and the characteristics that may challenge the process. If you're a Boomer, see which ones describe you. If you're not a Boomer, you should look anyway. You may be awarded honorary boomer status. Most of us are a mix of several categories, with a tendency to favor our "should fit" cohort. Use these four charts to select attributes that describe you. You may want to do further research on generational differences.

Traditionalists (1930-1945)	
Committed to hard work	Loyal and respectful of authority
Dedicated	Patriotic

Practical	Expect to make personal sacrifice
Respectful of authority	Expect hierarchy with top down management
Baby Boomers (1946-1964)	
Adaptive	Driven/live to work/ competitive, adaptive
Focused on individual choices and freedom	Love/hate relationship with authority
Goal-oriented	Prefers management by consensus
Optimistic, positive	Personal gratification building
accept diversity, emphasize team	Team, collaboration, avoids conflict
Generation X (1965-1976)	
Balanced/work to live, casual/technically literate	Focused on self
Unimpressed/not intimidated by authority	Reluctant to commit, independent
Expects leadership competence	Skeptical
Generation Y (1977-1990)	
Hopeful	Confident, can do attitude
Ambitious, want goals,	Seek meaningful work
Relaxed, polite, want to please authority	Need immediate feedback
Loyal	Achievers
Civic/ community awareness	Technologically proficient

Self-awareness is the key to successfully re-careering at all ages, including those of us older than 50. Your skill level is at its peak. You have a greater capacity for reflection than you did when you were younger. You are more emotionally mature than even 10 years ago. The more you understand and can describe these skills, the more you will see opportunities. Remember the *Keys to Your Future* as they apply here:

You are not looking for a job. Of course you want a job, but employers will hire you for what you bring to them, not what you need. Emphasizing what you bring to the job is especially important for older workers who may face age discrimination. Employers want people who can solve the problems they need solved. When you offer them that ability, you are in a position of strength.

The more you know the more you see. The better you understand what is important to you in the work that you do, the more opportunities you will see. As you gain experience you will be encouraged by the opportunities you see where you can help employers make money, save money, or look good.

Job security rests with knowing your skills, keeping them sharp, and knowing how to market them. The half-life of a new idea is about six months. You need to adapt your skills to embrace those new ideas as they emerge. The only thing that persists is your ability to solve problems.

Your enhanced self-awareness ties directly to your scanner-tuning efforts and the four scans:

- Scan your willingness to take responsibility for your career and your confidence that you can succeed. As you review your skills and the range of options for applying them, your self-confidence will increase.
- Scan your values, skills, and interest so that you know what matters to you. You can do a lot. Now look at those skills you prefer to use.
- Scan for information about your career and your willingness to seek out new learning experiences. You are entering a new country.

- Scan for opportunities to build mutually beneficial relationships. You know a lot of people and you have connections with a lot of different organizations. Strengthen and renew those now.

Most of us with 20 years or more of work will feel confident in most of those areas. As you review the skills, develop a narrative to describe yours. Completing this chart will be like reviewing the game film of your career. See what worked, what didn't work, and what you truly enjoyed.

Scan Skill: Skill area from "Areas of Experience and Maturity" list	
Experience	Where did you develop the skill? Some skills have grown as a result of multiple experiences, so you may want to break them out. You are tuning your scanner by reflecting on accomplishments, so you have flexibility in the way you fill the "experience" block. You use the writing process as a way to reflect on your experiences, so any work here will help with that introspection. As your introspection progresses, how to apply what you have learned from your experiences will become evident.
Achievement	What did you accomplish as a result of your experience? The more vivid your detail, the better you will increase your capacity to spot opportunities.
Benefit to a	As you develop resumes and

| company | conduct interviews, the data here will become selling points. |

Scan Skill: Communicate thoughts and idea s by writing and speaking.	
Experience	Multiple presentations at conferences and workshops.
Achievement	Invited to present at international conferences, multiple workshops in juried conferences.
Benefit to a company	Let potential buyers know about print materials available for purchase.

The more you can write about your use of this modified list of SCAN skills the more you can tune your scanner for employing your talents.

New Direction or the Familiar Path

As an experienced worker making career change during the late stage of your career, you might follow one three paths.

1. <u>Volunteering in an area that is new you or that uses the skills you've accumulated.</u> Multiple benefits come from volunteering beyond the obvious gains appreciated by your host. You can readily gain a sense of accomplishment, camaraderie, and new networks. Should you decide to return to paid employment your volunteer activities could pave the way. In any stage of life, volunteering is a natural way to scan for synergistic relationships and build your mutually beneficial networks.

2. <u>Minimum wage jobs might prove attractive as a way to stay active, add a little income, and avoid the pressures that might come with an occupation that uses your battery of skills</u>. Keep in mind one of our *keys: Every job makes money, saves money, or helps the company look good.*

Continue to build your resume and look for extra ways to support your part-time employer. The extra effort will build your feeling of accomplishment and may lead to opportunities to contribute more without compromising the reasons you left your career for part-time work in the first place.

3. <u>Staying on a traditional path is possible but has proven challenging for older workers thanks to age discrimination</u>. Many older workers out of a job have a tough time getting an equivalent position, especially if they are leaving a management post. Your experience also makes you more expensive. Productivity through technology means fewer new jobs, and they tend to be filled by younger workers. It can be daunting trying explain your value to a manager. However, the modest growth of new jobs is countered somewhat by the growth of small business.

4. <u>The growth in small business makes creating or working for a new enterprise a likely prospect for experienced workers.</u> You might return to a former employer as a consultant. You might consider purchasing an existing small business, expanding an avocational interest, creating something entirely new in order to fill a local need, or franchising. Review the chart below to see if your temperament is suited for entrepreneurship.

Entrepreneurs	**Non-entrepreneurs**
Thrive on risk	Are cautious and laid back
Enjoy the daily challenge and excitement of turning a profit	Prefer a steady paycheck and a predictable lifestyle
Prefer to be their own boss	Prefer direction from others

Are willing to invest a huge investment of hours and sacrifice	Are reluctant to invest a huge investment of hours and sacrifice
Are willing to assume considerable risk and can rebound from failure	Prefer the relative safety of being employed
Expect to put in long hours	Prefer a predictable schedule
Readily accept responsibility for themselves and others.	Are willing to assume limited responsibility for themselves and others
Accept being out there by themselves, with few mentors	Prefer having colleagues and camaraderie
Sacrifice "me" in order to focus on critical activities	Value free time and fit it into every day
Budget only goes to things that touch customers	Budget includes items for the person's comfort
Responsible for all tasks, from strategic planning to changing the printer ribbon	Delegate tasks
Invest in "must haves"	Invest in the latest and greatest
Work is life	Seek work–life balance
Everyday requires new contributions	Expect past accomplishments to allow a little coasting today

Few will come down completely on one side or the other. Age is also a factor, as older workers are less likely to cast their fate, and retirement savings, to a new roll of the dice. Small businesses and new, entrepreneurial efforts provide the most opportunity for re-careering Baby Boomers, so you might consider if your own business will yield satisfaction or a new kind of misery for you. If you believe you (and those around you, such as family members) are ready to take the plunge, complete the chart below. The ideas will help you focus on the outcomes and choices as you become the next Steve Jobs or establish the next Starbucks. Keep in mind, small businesses are risky. Consider LL Bean, who invented his famous boots and his unconditional guarantee in a small Maine store. He immediately sold 100 pairs. There was a problem with his glue and every pair came back. But he rebounded, adjusted his design, and turned his boots into a viable enterprise.

Gains expected from business ownership	Sacrifices expected from business ownership
Reasons my personality and attitude can help me succeed	Reasons my personality and attitude might limit my success
Family support I can expect	Family resistance to owning my own business
Business management, marketing, and financial skills I possess	Business management, marketing, and financial skills I need to learn

Franchises

According to Scott Balfour of Magnusson Balfour, a group of commercial and business brokers, franchises can cost from $25k to $40k. Some are strictly marketing franchises offering "brand names," while others are business franchises that have operating procedures, systems, and support. Turnkey programs may be attractive if you are getting into a new area. At first it's a nice way to run with things in place. But if you want to add creativity in the future, franchise restrictions may seem restrictive. With some franchises you may be signing a 10- or 15-year contract. If you go out of business you may be liable for any balances due the franchiser. If you want to transfer or sell the business, the process is generally controlled by the franchiser and often results in a diminished selling price. Plugging "franchise" into your web browser will yield a variety of sources on franchising. The web page for the International Franchise Association (http://www.franchise.org/) is a good place to start exploring. Be cautious, as always, when using Internet sites.

The three ideas explored here will help you tune your scanner and enhance self-awareness. Understanding the characteristics of your age group can help you understand your personality traits that can help a company solve business problems. Your capacity to describe your skills will help your "sales pitch" and focus on opportunities you might pursue. And if beginning a new enterprise is in the cards, your entrepreneurial efforts will come to the fore.

At this point, you may want to do or revisit *Activity Seven: Tuning Your Scanner with a Career Experience Timeline.*

William Stone, Ed.D. NCCC, President and CEO of Promising Futures

Bill received his doctorate from Vanderbilt University where he focused his research on career development. He holds a Certificate of Advanced Study from the University of Maine and B.S. and M.Ed. degrees from the University of Southern Maine. He is a National Certified Counselor (NCC) and a National Certified Career Counselor (NCCC). Bill worked as a high school guidance director and managed several grant-funded outreach programs. He also taught graduate courses in counselor education, especially on career-related topics, and co-authored *Beginning the Career Exploration System* and *The Career Exploration System,* published by AGS. He focused on the science of chaos theory and careers as the guest editor of the issue of the *Career Planning and Adult Development Journal.* Before becoming President and CEO of Promising Futures, Bill was Clinical Director of the Higher Education Resources Outreach program (HERO) for the Maine Education Services Foundation. You can view his LinkedIn page to learn more and connect.

www.ingramcontent.com/pod-product-compliance
Lightning Source LLC
LaVergne TN
LVHW051118080426
835510LV00018B/2102